Praise for Kare
and *The Styleprint*

"Karen Powell unselfishly lays out not only the trade secrets to redecorating and redefining your living space, she gives you the worksheets to do it! This is a must-read for anyone that wants to sharpen and quicken their learning curve when it comes to redecorating at any level of complexity!"

—**Melanie Bergeron**, CFE, chair of the board, Two Men and a Truck; International Franchise Association, 2015 chair

"*The Styleprint Design System* takes what can be the overwhelming task of redecorating and breaks things down into simple planning steps. To have worksheets that help you organize your decisions along the way and are then there for review throughout the process is genius!"

—**Rosemarie Hartnet**, CFE, president, Abrakadoodle

"What a relief! Through this book, Karen Powell has made the overwhelming task of decorating completely manageable and enjoyable. Professionals as well as newbies to decorating will benefit from this straightforward, progressive, and completely doable approach to decorating. Dig in, and you will be excited by all the opportunities that lie ahead of you!"

—**Doreen Banaszak**, dbcoaching

"*The StylePrint Design System* provides an excellent road map for creating beautiful spaces that people love to live in. This common sense, step-by-step system takes the guesswork—and the stress—out of decorating. I use this system with all of my clients!"

—**Amy Boesen**, CID, certified color specialist, Decor&You franchisee, decorating design coach, former chair of advisory council, interim vendor relations liaison, member of the D&Y education team.

"Karen is a professional who turned her passion into her career. Our homes are our place of safety, enjoyment, and rejuvenation. Deciding to take on a decorating project in a home can interrupt our sanctuary. Karen gives us a safety net to finally fix that space that has bothered us for too long and bring emotional enjoyment back into our home's design!"

—**Ed Schultek**, founder and managing partner, Sandler Training/Peak Sales Performance

"Finally! A personal blueprint everyone can easily use to create the best in their home. Long overdue! Well done, Karen."

—**Nancy Friedman**, speaker and president, Telephone Doctor Customer Service Training

"I pleaded, I begged, I even made that face (you know the one) to get her not to include trademarked information, but Karen was insistent on sharing the inner secrets to decorating gleaned over her thirty years of education, experience, and sometimes excruciating business lessons. *The StylePrint Design System* is the one book that takes the decorating and design training you previously couldn't obtain without a significant investment of time and money and marries it with practical business formulas that deliver a business you can not only love but one that delivers bottom line results.

If you are a decorator in training, a hobby decorator, or a decorator/designer that loves the home fashions industry yet struggles with practical business dollars and sense (not measly cents!) this book may boost your passion and your P&L."

—**Linda T Gottlieb**, MA, CFE, director of education,
Decor&You

"The anatomy of a decor project and *The Styleprint Design System* created by Karen Powell is thought provoking while instilling confidence that we can all be active and successful participants in designing the work or home environment we would love."

—**Art Mulligan**, insurance and finance advisor
and business owner

"I thought *The Styleprint Design System* was very practical and concrete. It is not meant to be a quick fix solution book. It requires serious thought and consideration of the situation and the process. The reader has to really think about what he/she has and what he/she wants and how to accomplish it. It can be time consuming. One of the features I liked best in the book were the personal examples; they make it easier to understand."

—**Janice Walsh**, business educator and coach

"Karen wrote this book for me! I am a lifelong 'do-it-your-selfer' decorator with many 'it seemed like a good idea at the time' decorator projects under my belt and at various levels of completion. The only word I can use to describe *The Styleprint Design System* is WOW! The information in this book, presented in Karen's comfortable, helpful, 'let's chat over a cup of coffee or a glass of wine' style, wowed me by its down-to-earth, logical, 'I now feel empowered,' step-by-step process to transform the spaces I call home into a space and place that is a true reflection of me, my lifestyle, my place to work, live, entertain, relax, and rejuvenate. I'm excited to have this tool in my 'do-it-myself' decorator toolbox as I look to tackling projects in my twelve-year-old home."

> —**Joan Marlow**, life and wellness coach, educator, long-time associate and friend of Karen Powell

"Decor&You has really changed the world of decorating by simplifying the overwhelming task of decorating. They have taken the fear out of decorating and differentiated themselves in a way that I have not seen in over 25 years of franchising. Approaching the market in a way that gives their clients the confidence they need to create the space they dream of with Styleprint is nothing short of brilliant."

> —**Susan Stilwell**, franchising executive

"Magical! Creative use of space, lovely choices of room colors and furniture options. Flows! Love our home!"

> —**Judy Miller**, D&Y client, medical professional

"Do not read this book if you're expecting some theoretical treatise on interior design. This book is full of practical, hands-on advice on how to decorate a room in a simple but elegant manner. Using the step-by-step Styleprint Design System, you'll turn frustration into fascination when you see just how easily you can produce a finished product like the pros! Karen has a way of making things easy. If you've ever seen a room designed by Karen's Decor&You team, you'll instantly understand their tag line of 'Love the space you're in.' This book is a must read for anyone who wants to decorate and hear the inevitable, 'Wow!'"

—**Brian K. Miller**, CFE, COO, Patrice & Associates, Franchising, Inc., and franchise industry expert

"Karen Powell, an icon in the decorating and franchising industries, has written this simple step-by-step book to take the mystery and angst out of home decorating. Your home will become the envy of friends and family by using Karen's advice to create a beautiful living environment."

—**Mary Ellen Sheets**, founder, Two Men and A Truck, first woman recipient of the International Franchise Association's Entrepreneur of the Year Award, 2004

"I thoroughly enjoyed reading Karen's book. It's easy to understand, flows beautifully, and addresses immediately the key challenges we all face at the onset of a project. I love the way she breaks the information down into digestible components. And she's right, a new home or a re-do project can quickly become overwhelming. Her system provides a way to manage/control the physical as well as psychological processes at work.

I also like the way she introduces the benefits of bringing a design professional into the mix. It's very low key/low pressure but highlights what an experienced eye and objective perspective can bring to bear. Perfectly balanced. And will be well received.

My daughter struggles with a small house, tiny/dark rooms, and a growing family. Those little rooms were fine when her daughter and son were babies, but now there are real challenges.

I envision her being gripped by the possibilities of the worksheets and upcoming chapters. She is bright, creative, and imaginative, however, she has looked at the house and its inner space for so many years, its difficult to envision new options and potential. And although both she and her husband are professionals, their resources are limited. So on all levels, Karen's words resonate. It's given me plenty to think of in my own home as well."

—**Laura Collins**, HR professional and entrepreneur

"I found *The Styleprint® Design System* a delightful, fun and informative read. It is essential for the novice as well as the experienced Designer or Decorator. There is something to be learned at every turn to enhance your overall project experience."

—**Jane Cyr**, Vendor Relations Liaison at Decor&You

"Wish this book was available the first and every time I've decorated. It's a simple, easy, and clear way to have space that is "me". With this as my guide, I can't wait to tackle the next project!"

—**Ross Slater**, Entrepreneurial Coach, Reach Capabilities

"Karen Powell has developed a proven simple system for a complicated topic, interior design. Her knowledge, experience, and passion helping people fulfill their desires for the space where they live has brought many smiles and warmth to homes across America. This book allows for this gift from Karen to continue on for many generations."

—**Art Coley, Jr.**, CFE, President and CEO, Franchise Source Brands International®

THE

STYLEPRINT®

DESIGN

SYSTEM

KAREN POWELL

THE
STYLEPRINT®
DESIGN
SYSTEM

CREATED BY **DECOR&YOU** DESIGN GROUP

Published by Advantage, Charleston, South Carolina.
Member of Advantage Media Group.

ADVANTAGE is a registered trademark and the Advantage colophon is a trademark of Advantage Media Group, Inc.

Printed in the United States of America.

ISBN: 978-1-59932-463-0
LCCN: 2015952494

Book design by Megan Elger.

This publication is designed to provide accurate and authoritative information in regard to the subject matter covered. It is sold with the understanding that the publisher is not engaged in rendering legal, accounting, or other professional services. If legal advice or other expert assistance is required, the services of a competent professional person should be sought.

Advantage Media Group is proud to be a part of the Tree Neutral® program. Tree Neutral offsets the number of trees consumed in the production and printing of this book by taking proactive steps such as planting trees in direct proportion to the number of trees used to print books. To learn more about Tree Neutral, please visit **www.treeneutral.com**. To learn more about Advantage's commitment to being a responsible steward of the environment, please visit **www.advantagefamily.com/green**

Advantage Media Group is a publisher of business, self-improvement, and professional development books and online learning. We help entrepreneurs, business leaders, and professionals share their Stories, Passion, and Knowledge to help others Learn & Grow. Do you have a manuscript or book idea that you would like us to consider for publishing? Please visit **advantagefamily.com**.

DEDICATION

To all who have helped make my dream of creating a professional opportunity in a fun, dynamic, and impactful industry real:

My husband, Terry.

My daughter, Pamela.

My parents, Garry and Shirley Mitchell.

My business and design mentors: Mary Gilliatt, JoAnn Brezette.

My team: Linda Gottlieb, Dawn Ingala, Jane Cyr, Kris Gumbulevich, Dianne Sannella, Heather Palmer, Janice Walsh, Kim Ambrosio, Susan Scotts, Chris Otter, Susan Stilwell, Patrick Conley, Paul Pieschel, Brian Miller, Cory Denninger.

My Franchise Source Brands International (FSBI) sister team members: Tamara Loring, Marissa Ruderman, Kathleen Pugliese, Alexandria Watson, Jessica Pettit, Art Coley, Jenny Langfeld, Tony Perugini, Dylan Maher, Bill Michael.

My franchisee partners and their teams: Amy Boesen, Sandra Hambley (Janet Aurora, Katie McGovern, Crystal Cline, Bonnie Peet, Gina Simpson), Paul Allegro, Linnore Gonzales (Jen Linder, Linda O'Brien, Laura Gooding, Imani Celestin), Therese Bush-Hilgar, Kelly Murphy, Carleen DeSisto, Dana Petrie, Jenny Velasquez, Patty Lustig, Joanne LaRiccia, Robin Hebert, Kayla Johns, Jean Vonglis, Liane Rigano, Janine Smith, Carol Grote, Lenore Congemi, Leslie Klinck.

Our key product partners: Kincaid Furniture, Bill Hairston, and Max Dyer; Klaussner Furniture, Tony Bellarosa; Hunter Douglas, Larry Nover; Lafayette, Christy Kerrigan; Surya; Global Views; Uttermost, Gale Egan; Mary McCauley; David Ash.

ACKNOWLEDGMENTS

The following people have been instrumental in my career path and the creating of Decor&You, the opportunity that educates and offers The Styleprint Design System so that anyone can love the space they are in.

Mary Gilliatt, an icon in the home furnishings industry. Her career spans over 5 decades, across oceans. She is the author of over 40 books, including *Mary Gilliatt's Interior Design Course*, which she authored after she wrote the Mary Gilliatt Design Course for the Decor&You franchise organization. In addition, she has decorated numerous homes from New York City to London to France and New Zealand, which also included some celebrity homes. She is not only a valued mentor and colleague, she is a friend.

JoAnn Brezette, an industry guru, trainer, and author in the window fashions world. JoAnn taught me most of what I know about window coverings and has educated many of the

Decor&You franchise owners and decorators. Her book, *Selling to the Limit,* is the first required reading for all of our franchisees and their decorators. JoAnn has a very personable, no-nonsense business approach to beautiful window coverings and homes with style. I am honored to be associated with her and to call her a friend as well.

Bill Hairston, an icon in the furniture segment of the home fashions industry. Bill has shared his wisdom and expertise with me and all of Decor&You since we began our franchise. We are honored to have him associated with us—he is a friend as well as a professional colleague.

Ed Schultek of the Sandler Sales System has been a committed partner of Decor&You for many years. He has passionately and patiently educated us all on how to become the trusted advisor for our clients that we know they want. You can sign up for his insightful newsletter at www.peakperformancesales.com.

Terry Powell, my husband, marketing guru, and franchise visionary. He was the first one instrumental for me to act on my entrepreneurial vision and ability. It was his encouragement that enabled me to launch into a career of business ownership and creating a franchise opportunity.

The mentors, colleagues, professionals, and friends at **TransDesigns**, Woodstock, GA, from 1984–1994, a decorating company which was my entry into the world of decor. It has been fun to learn and grow in this marvelous industry.

Doreen Banaszak, author of *Excuse Me Your Life Is Now* and *The Power of Acceptance*, Conscious Creator, for her insightful perspective and coaching on how to get more of what I want in life and to have fun doing it!

Verne Harnish, author of *The Rockefeller Habits* and producer of the Fortune 500 Leadership Summit and Growth Summit, amazing events of current and forward-thinking thought leadership in the world of business and abundance.

My friends at Strategic Coach—**Dan Sullivan**, **Babs Smith**, **Shannon Waller**, and **Ross Slater**— for their fabulous coaching/systems and tools for entrepreneurs to get beyond their ceiling of complexity and achieve results better, faster, easier, and cheaper. *Ross worked with me to define our unique process, The Styleprint Design System.*

Dina Dwyer-Owens, CFE, Co-Chair the Dwyer Group, Inc., mentor, colleague, and friend in franchising. Thank you for your guidance, wisdom, and for introducing me to Strategic Coach.

Franchise owners and **Styleprint DecorDesigners** with the Decor&You organization. Thank you for embarking on creating and developing your businesses and careers with me. It is amazingly joyful to participate in your success. I am also extremely proud of the work you all do as showcased by a few in the photos in this book which come from real people that are your clients and assisting them in loving the space they are in!

CONTENTS

 *FOREWORD*

I have written 43 books on various aspects of decorating over the course of 50 years, and as a result, I often receive letters asking for help and advice. But nothing could have prepared me for the avalanche of mail I received when my PBS series *Decorating with Mary Gilliatt*, the first TV decorating series in the US and UK, aired in 1990.

As I reviewed these letters, I was struck by the number of people who feared a decorator would ignore and override their own tastes. I had never even considered that before. I always thought some people were born with innate decorating confidence, but most would profit from a framework with a range of choices to customize each project. In other words, a series of recipes that they could "spice up" their own way.

The realization made me start a number of projects, including designing and photographing examples of rooms done in various styles suitable for differing types of homes to provide inspiration, and then bringing together professional decorators of all talent levels from all over the States and training them in all the ways the catalog, schemes, and styles could be used according to budgets.

I had a business plan in place, and my team was starting to raise funding to get started when, out of the blue, I received a call from Karen Powell.

Karen's customary efficiency had got there first and far more simply. She and her then partner had had many if not all of the same ideas, especially their own decorators from all over the country with their fail-safe system (or recipe) but, most importantly, her company, which she had registered with the name of Decor&You, was designed to be a franchise, something I had not even thought of, and which, of course, more or less raised its own funding. Would I like to join as design consultant? I did.

Twenty-five years later, with all the wisdom and experience collated from Decor&You's very large number of satisfied customers all over the States, Karen has written her own book explaining her very own Styleprint Design System, her own design recipe book for success. It is a great tool for finding and using your own style in a way you might never have thought possible.

Mary Gilliatt, *industry icon in home and commercial decor*

Karen has been passionate about business and entrepreneurship from her early days of working in an office, followed by a ten-year stint as a secondary business education teacher, and then creating her own business, first through an association with a decorating company, TransDesigns, and then creating her own company and opportunity in the home furnishings industry, Decor&You. She franchised Decor&You in 1998 with the vision to provide an opportunity to others who enjoyed the field of decorating and who also wanted to be masters of their own destiny and yet appreciated a system and colleagues to collaborate with.

The mission of Decor&You is to delight our clients with their environments so that they, *"Love the space they are in,"* whether that be home, office, or commercial setting. We love compliments that tell us: "Wow! I absolutely love my room—and I never would have made those choices without you!" That's how we know we have done our job and done it well!

Karen lives in Connecticut with her husband Terry and their two bichon frises, Gizmo and Toby. In the summer she spends time with her family at the Jersey Shore.

 *INTRODUCTION*

FROM COMPLEX TO SIMPLE—THE ANATOMY OF A DECOR PROJECT

When it comes to *decorating*, most people get overwhelmed before they even get started.

They run wildly from room to room with a dozen paint chips in their hands and wind up getting nowhere but frustrated.

Or worse: they go out and start shopping. Paint, couches, and carpets roll in, and then they realize it's still not looking good. Embarrassment settles in on top of the frustration.

Or even worse: they watch a few do-it-yourself shows, start ripping into a total room remodel, and quickly find out that there is a lot more going on behind the scenes to complete a project.

Typically, every seven to twelve years, it happens all over again. That's when people tend to have a change in their lives or get tired of their surroundings.

When you buy a new home, you redecorate. If you have a child, you're bound to redecorate. You finish the basement … time to decorate. The kids grow up and want a bedroom makeover … you redecorate again. And when the kids go off to college or get married, it's a good time to take a look around and redo some things. Then, at some point, you think about downsizing because the house is a lot to keep up.

Your Home 2.0 will help you identify whether tackling a decor project makes sense. *Your Home 2.0* is a one-page document designed to help you think about your space to determine your level of discomfort with that space and identify, in broad terms, just what it is that's bugging you so that you can set goals for improvement.

The truth is, with a proven, step-by-step system and a helping hand when you need it, you *can* overcome your home's challenges—and your own worries—to create the spaces of your dreams. And when it's time to redecorate again, you'll know how to do it right the first time.

This book is the first step … well, the first five steps, actually. Page by page, you will discover how to turn your own unique design preferences into a reality, something we call a Styleprint®. Your style, much like your fingerprint, is yours and yours alone.

YOUR HOME 2.0™

DECOR&YOU®
LOVE THE SPACE YOU'RE IN

Why not create a Styleprint® for the place you know you deserve?

If you look at your space a year from now, what has to happen for you to think it is beautiful and comfortable?

DATE		
	RENT OWN	NEW
NAME		
EMAIL		
PHONE		

Karen Powell
Decor&You® CEO & Founder
203.405.2123 kpowell@decorandyou.com

I HATE IT: You walk into your space; it's not comfortable, functional or beautiful.
Check next to the areas that are unsatisfactory in your home and add others if needed.

- ✓ Walls
- Floors
- Ceiling
- Furniture
- Lighting
- Window Treatments
- Wall Art
- Accessories
- Color Scheme
- Floor Planning

FRUSTRATIONS	GOALS
From the decorating dilemmas please note the 3 top frustrations and fill in your goals	

I NEED TO CHANGE IT: If you had a magic wand, your next decorating design project would start here.
Check next to the areas that really need attention and add others if needed.

- Room Flow
- Green Friendly
- New Furniture
- More Time
- Color harmony
- Updated Feel
- Suits Lifestyle
- Curb Appeal
- Better Lighting
- Window Treatments

PROJECTS	GOALS
From the decorating projects please note the 3 top and fill in your goals	

I LOVE IT: You may have a place in your home that feels complete with pieces you love.
Put an X next to what you love about your space and add others if needed.

- Focal Point
- Artwork
- Treasures
- View
- Architectural Design
- Floor Plan/Function
- Feel/Comfort
- Color Pallet
- Furniture
- Drapery

LOVE IT	GOALS
From the things you love please note the 3 top loves and fill in your goals	

Take it from me. It works! I've spent 30 years as a DecorDesigner and am, currently, the creator, founder, and owner of Decor&You®, a nationwide decorating design business. All of our professional DecorDesigners use the Styleprint Design System as the foundation of their many tools to help clients. Now you are armed with the tools that real professionals use.

The Styleprint Design System distills everything that I have learned along my journey in decorating design. My education and training came through immersing myself in the industry: reading books, taking workshops and seminars, asking questions of professionals and product partners, being mentored, and assessing the dilemmas of all my clients in search of options that would truly solve their problem and make them smile. One mentor, Mary Gilliatt, has proven especially invaluable to me. She is an international icon in the industry and has written over 40 decorating books. She is not only a trusted professional but also a friend. Much of my initial knowledge and refinement of that knowledge came from her.

HOW TO GET STARTED

The anatomy of a decor project is a sequence of thoughts and actions that begins with something that is "off." Some people call it a pain point. No matter how large or small, each project relies on the following steps, known as the Styleprint Design System:

Step 1: Styleprint Discovery

- Define what is "off," and describe the problem it's causing.

- Develop a vision of the desired end result.

- Form a diagnosis and ask what will correct it.

- Examine the physical space; outline personal preferences.

Step 2: The Style Success Survey

- Complete the survey to explore and confirm your original diagnosis.

Step 3: Possibilities Creation

- Research and prepare solutions in detail for consideration, ranked by personal criteria (a.k.a. treatment plan).

- Review solution options.

- Select a plan.

Step 4: The Managed Makeover

- Implement the plan details.

- Evaluate the solution: did you solve the problem?

- Repeat the steps until you are satisfied.

Step 5: The Styleprint Showcase

- Take photos, share, and enjoy.

This five-step system needs your input to work. As you complete the short worksheet exercises included in this book, you'll begin to define your style and build a practical look, feel, and function around it that you will absolutely love.

The Styleprint Design System starts with Styleprint discovery, in which you explore your decorating challenges, preferences, and priorities. In the second step, you complete the Style Success Survey by going through your room and systematically assessing the space. The survey helps to evaluate your design needs and cultivate your Styleprint. Perhaps you're interested in design choices that are safe and healthy for your family and the environment. Or maybe you feel your space lacks cohesion or fails to reflect your personality.

By the time you get to the third step, possibilities creation, you'll see your room's design potential unfold before your eyes. Based on your Styleprint and the space, you'll start to consider samples, swatches, and sketches to bring the possibilities to life. Because you've done the earlier steps, everything is tailored to your investment level and your unique needs. Choose your favorites or mix and match details to create your dream look. By the time you complete the final steps—the managed makeover and the Styleprint showcase—you will be able to sit back and enjoy a brand new room that looks good, feels right, and functions the way you want. It's ready to live in and love.

You are ready to get started with the tools you need to confidently discover your own Styleprint and design the space that you've been wanting. If you get stuck, let us know, and our experts will work with you to craft a distinctive look that feels right for you. Consider us your go-to home decor resource. We're here for you.

Visit us at www.styleprintdesignsystem.com for the downloadable worksheets and to send us your questions.

CHAPTER ONE

STEP 1: STYLEPRINT DISCOVERY

Before you can have a home filled with rooms that wow you, you must focus on what you want. How is each piece of the puzzle going to fit into the whole? Once you understand your goals for your home and each room, it's easier to address the challenges in front of you. If decorating is a struggle for you, you're not alone. Many people get overwhelmed, feel unsure of themselves, and get tired of seeing the same thing everywhere they go or displayed in magazines. But it all becomes easier and more manageable when you follow a system.

As Steven Covey writes in *Seven Habits of Highly Effective People*, the way to begin is to start with the end in mind, habit number two.

THE IMPORTANCE OF LOOKING AHEAD

The Styleprint discovery stage first identifies something that is not right. As you begin to contemplate this, begin with the end in mind. Essentially, you think about what you want the outcome to be, as opposed to purchasing odd items of decor such as a piece of furniture, an accessory, or a rug, and seeing what happens from there. When you start without knowing where you want to go, things go downhill fast. What works time after time is to start with where you want to end up and work backward from there. The counterintuitive part here is that you may start with one piece of furniture or art or a color that you love and build around it. There is a difference between consciously selecting something that you love and using it as the inspiration for the rest of the room and aimlessly selecting something because it strikes you at the moment.

Looking at the process from the perspective of the desired result helps you to focus and think about the look, feel, and function of the room. You must be happy with all three of those criteria in order to declare the project a success in the end. If it looks good but doesn't feel good and doesn't function for you—it doesn't work. You will be annoyed and irritated living with it. That's not the purpose of your space. Each room in your home is expected to support your life. Consider your home the theatrical stage where your life unfolds. It's a place where you can rest, relax, and rejuvenate. It's also where you celebrate, entertain, and get together with others. Or it's a place where you work. Your environment plays a supporting role in whatever you're doing in your life.

To begin the process, identify something that doesn't feel right or is missing. Is it an item? Is it a color? Is it the whole room? Describe it in three sentences or less. How complex is it? Is it something for which purchasing one item will make all the difference, or is it more intricate than that?

The solution could be as simple as hanging your favorite piece of art on the wall over the sofa, adding greenery in a corner of the room to round it out, or anchoring the room with a beautiful area rug. Or it could be more complex: the entire color theme may be lacking in personality and placement, in which case adding a wall covering, pillows, and coordinated accessories may do the trick by pulling out colors from the area rug, art, and upholstered furnishings. Or the room may simply not be lit in a way that enhances its style and function and therefore does not feel good or inviting. To remedy this, general lighting may be the best enhancement.

After identifying your pain point, focus on what you want to accomplish by making a change and why. Make notes on your vision of the completed project. What does it look like? Be specific. Consider the end result: what will a change do for the room and for your enjoyment and use of that room? Consider the opposite as well: what will it mean to you if you do not make any enhancements?

For assistance with this thought process, go to www.styleprintdesignsystem.com, download Worksheet #1 ("Focus Step"), and listen to the podcast that walks you through the thinking involved in filling the worksheet out. You will also find a copy of all the Worksheets in the Appendix in the back of this book.

When it comes to decorating, what seems logical often is not, and what seems illogical often actually is.

When it comes to decorating, what seems logical often is not, and what seems illogical often actually is.

To gain clarity, ask yourself questions and discover your challenges: What are your preferences? What are your priorities? These become the building blocks to work through those challenges and to uncover your unique design, your Styleprint.

MAKING DISCOVERIES THROUGH ANALYSIS

Styleprint discovery encompasses more than one level of detailed analysis. On Worksheet #1, "Focus Step," you identify what your decorating dilemma is, what you want to accomplish, and why. In addition, you elaborate on your vision of the completed project with three criteria that the finished project must include for you to consider it a successful venture.

Worksheet #2 ("Evaluate Your Space") has you take a critical eye to the details of the room. To do this, you will review each aspect of the room through the lens of how well each supports the room's function and how well the physical space and your personal preferences accommodate the desired function—not how much you like each part of the room but how well each part supports or does not support the overall function you desire. Refer to Worksheet #2 ("Evaluate Your Space") at www.styleprintdesignsystem.com or in the Appendix.

As you continue your evaluation, move into the room and consider how well the arrangement of furnishings works in relationship to the scale of the room and its function. Do you need different or more pieces to enhance the function? Eventually, you will draw a room arrangement plan to establish which size of furniture will work and to make sure you can move about easily.

Finally, critically review the overall aesthetics and the look and feel of the room. Does the room make you smile? Does it invite you in? Make some notes about how it makes you feel and how much it appeals to your aesthetic sense. Later, you will consider options for completing the look of your space. This is very similar to enhancing the look of a little black dress: it's a nice enough dress as it is, but when you see it accessorized, it transforms into "Wow! I need that!"

Once you have completed your analysis, determine whether you are ready and willing to make any of the major changes. You want to complete these first.

As you evaluate how well the space is or is not meeting your criteria, start by asking yourself the following questions:

Function of the space:

- Who will use this room? For what purpose? How often?

- Tell us about the room as it is now. What works, and what doesn't?

- What is your vision for this room?

Physical characteristics of the space:

- What is your overall impression of the room? What is the room's best feature? What is one thing about the room that annoys you?

- Do the colors work for you?

- Does the room accommodate its function?

- What type of natural light does the room get? What are the wired lighting options?

- What works now, and what may need to be replaced or added in these areas:

  - ☐ walls

  - ☐ floors

  - ☐ ceiling

  - ☐ furniture

  - ☐ window treatments

  - ☐ artwork

  - ☐ accessories

  - ☐ storage

- What else is there to note about the room?

- On the personal side, there are preferences to be considered:

  - ☐ Color, contrast, or subtle flow of color? Color families?

- ☐ Tailored, crisp look, or intricate detail with layers?

- ☐ Wood? Fabric? Texture?

- ☐ Natural light? Privacy?

- ☐ Special needs?

- ☐ How is comfort defined?

There is a column on the worksheet for inputting the financial investment that you are willing to make to create the space. If you don't want to commit to a dollar amount now, skip that column and come back to it later when you are researching solutions. Ultimately, however, how much you are willing to invest will be a major factor in your final selections, your solutions. Keep in mind that some solutions will affect your home's value, so you may decide to put more dollars into the solution than originally planned.

For example, if you eliminate old kitchen fluorescent lights and add in pendant lighting, overhead fixtures, and a chandelier, you may improve the resale value of your home by thousands of dollars. This change may more than pay back your investment when you sell your home and assist you in selling your home more quickly because of the fresh, updated look.

When you move into a new home, you may love it or love parts of it, you may accept it for what it is, or you may just not like it. It's all personal, and it's hard to see the forest for the trees. You don't see the beauty of the home, and you also don't see what's missing for you. This is where an objective third party can be helpful. This book is designed to guide you just as a professional would if that professional were in the room with you. The desired outcome is that you love your home, with *your own* look, *your own* feel, and *your own* function—your Styleprint. Given the physical parameters of your space, take the principles and elements of good design, along with your preferences and priorities, and mix them all together. That's how the magic is created. You will know you have hit your goal when you think, *Wow! I absolutely love my home!*

After you determine what is "off," assess what you have. Begin from the outside in. As you enter a room, critique it. Look at its size, its shape, and where the light sources are, both natural and artificial. Look at the colors and the permanent features.

- Is there a fireplace? Is it brick? Is it stone? What color?

- Is there cabinetry? Color? Accents?

- Is there a hardwood floor? What color? What condition is it in?

- Is there wall-to-wall carpeting? What color? Is it in good condition?

- How about the walls? Are they rustic logs, brick, stucco, or wallpapered?

- Standard ceiling height?

- Any architectural features?

Once you have evaluated the structure of the room, determine what you like and do not like about it. For each thing that you don't like, do you have the ability—meaning the time, investment resources, or patience—to change it? As an example, transforming a carpeted room to hardwood flooring is a major project. All the furniture must be moved out, the carpet ripped up and disposed of, and hardwood either installed or refinished. This could take several days and is inconvenient. Are you ready for the sacrifice?

My own home had a fireplace that the previous owners loved, but it just didn't fit with my personal preferences. The hearth was high. The mantel was high. The brick was not a charming red brick that I could work with. Every time I attempted to create a family room in that space, I got stuck; I couldn't pull together anything that I liked. Ultimately, I realized that no matter how much money I put into everything else in that room, the fireplace was always going to be a sticking point. It was time for an alternative solution.

Rather than painting the brick, which wasn't going to give me the wow effect I was after, I spoke with a contractor, and we brainstormed how to alter it. The final solution was to put plywood over the top part of the brick, paint it, and put marble trim around the fireplace opening, with glass doors, to eliminate the brick completely. It wasn't as expensive as I thought it would be, and it gave me the ability to create the room that I really wanted.

Photo courtesy of Janet Aurora, Styleprint Designer, Hambley Team

LIGHTING THE WAY

Lighting is often an undervalued part of the decorating process, and yet it sets the tone—the function, the look, and the feel—for everything else. Typically, when people start to think about making changes or even at the very beginning of creating a room, they will jump into the color, the furnishings and their placement, and then the accessories, along with other finishing touches. It is usually at the time of putting the finishing touches in place that someone will begin to think about the lighting. "Gee, is there an outlet near where I want to put that lamp?" or "How much light do I really need in this room? How do I know?" Often, what is left to last is best considered first. And it is better to plan for more lighting than needed because you can always turn something off. Ideally, plan to light the room first based on how you will utilize it. That way, you will have outlets—and enough of them—where you need them. Also, consider general or overhead lighting for every space. It's better to not use lighting later on than not have what you need, because lighting is so important!

THE STYLEPRINT® DESIGN SYSTEM
TECHNICAL DÉCOR INFO: LIGHTING

4 types of light:

Natural	General/Ambient
Task	Accent/Ambience/Mood

Ideal: Have all four types in the room

Tip: Use dimmers wherever possible to be able to control the light for best application

Light affects color

Exposure:	Northern = adds blue
	Eastern = adds yellow or green
	Southern = adds yellow-white; neutralizes
	Western = adds orange
Time of day:	Varying effect on color
Artificial light:	*Fluorescent light*— enhances blues/greens; mutes reds/yellows
	Halogen light—best replaces natural light; doesn't distort color; white
	Incandescent light – warmer tones enhanced; cool tones dulled
Shades effect:	Shade color will project its color into the room; Opaque shade directs light out the top and bottom; Translucent shade lets out light.

Guidelines for sizing of fixtures:

How to calculate the proper size of a Ceiling Fixture:
Width:
   Room Length (ft) + Room width (ft) =
   _____ Ceiling Fixture width in inches

Height:
   minimum 7' from the floor

Diameter of chandelier over a table:
   table width – 12" = diameter

Height of chandelier over table:
   30" above table (8' ceiling)

Sconces:
   placed 5' up from floor; min. 28" apart

Table lamp:
   shade at eye level of person seated
   proportionate to table and room

Vanity light over mirror:
   minimum 24" wide

The Styleprint Design System considers light from four different perspectives:

1. What is the reaction of the people who live in the space? How do they feel about its light?

2. How much natural light is there? Natural daylight makes a big difference. What are the exposure, number, and type of windows? Note the surroundings outside the home. If you live in a city where the buildings are

almost up against each other, that affects the amount of natural daylight. Or if you live out in the country and it's hilly, it may take longer for natural light to fill the rooms because the sun is rising behind the hills, or in the evening the sun may set earlier because it's behind the trees. But at the shore, you may get the full effect of daylight from sunrise to sunset.

Photo courtesy of Therese Bush-Hilgar, Styleprint Designer

3. What types of artificial light are available in the room: general, mood, task? This will affect the look, feel, and function of the room. Lighting touches every aspect of decor.

The artificial sources available are:

☐ overhead: chandeliers, fixtures close to the ceiling, and recessed—for general light

☐ lamps: floor, table, and desk—for tasks

☐ sconces: for general or ambience light, depending on the number in a room

☐ small (often concealed) transmitters of light: candles or canisters placed as uplights under cabinetry and concealed in molding—for ambience or mood

4. What exists now, and what is still needed for the maximum enjoyment of the room? This question is important because lighting sets the stage for the entire room and how everything in it is viewed. It can also be tricky, as many people are not well versed in the different types of lighting and how to get the most from them. More about this later.

When evaluating lighting within a room, first determine its purpose:

☐ Is it task lighting (lighting needed to perform a task, whether to read, knit, or cook)?

- ☐ Is it general lighting (the overall illumination in a room)?

- ☐ Is it ambient/mood lighting?

Each lighting function plays an important role in the overall design of the room. Let's assess the dining room, for example. This is a place where you need general lighting, but it's also a place where your focus is on the task of eating. At the same time, you may want some ambiance, some mood lighting in that room. The overall lighting could be provided by a chandelier, natural light through a window, or wall sconces that provide lighting around the room's perimeter. Put the sconces on dimmers, and you can change the lighting with the touch of your finger to create more mood or ambiance. After dinner you might decide that you want more subtle light in the room. The chandelier could have tiers of individual bulbs that can be turned on or off.

Photo courtesy of Janet Aurora, Styleprint Designer, Hambley Team

Remember to keep the function of the space in mind. This will dictate how you light up a room. In a family room, you might use recess lights over the sofa area and put them on a dimmer switch. This allows for sitting and watching TV when you do not want much light.

WORKING WITH WHAT YOU HAVE

Decorating focuses first on the elements of good design, and everything flows from that perspective. These elements are:

- light
- color
- texture and pattern
- scale and balance

Within each element, there are choices to make. This is where personal preferences, quality, level of investment, and other intangible elements come into play. There are, inevitably, crossroads where you will make decisions based on the amount of time, energy, and dollars you have allocated for a particular project.

For example, I worked with a client we'll call Sally. When I arrived, she had moved into a previously occupied condo that was unfurnished. She had a budget and an idea of what to do first. Her thought was to rip out all the carpet and put in new carpeting. This was a five-room condo, and doing that would have eaten up a big chunk of her budget. There was nothing wrong with the carpet; it was in good condition. But it was neutral in color, and Sally wanted color. She felt the carpet was ugly.

Photo courtesy of Crystal Cline, Styleprint Designer, Hambley Team

Because the carpet still had value from a professional's perspective, I considered how else to put color into Sally's home. If she changed the carpet, she would have less to invest in furnishings. One consideration was to add color in other areas of the room: the window treatments—which she would need for privacy and light control—wall coverings, or paint, plus some nice artwork, accessories, and an area rug.

We selected items with colors, patterns, and texture to complete the room layout. Sally got excited about the plan and forgot about replacing the carpet. Once it was all together, she absolutely loved her new home, and she was tickled to still have some invest-ment dollars to spend on other things. Ultimately, it meant we were able to decorate several rooms instead of having to do the whole condo in stages.

Photo courtesy of
Amy Boesen,
Styleprint Designer

When you walk into an empty room and all you see is the carpet, it's easy to think, *Oh my gosh! I want to replace this ugly carpet!* If you have the budget and desire to make the replacement, that may be the right direction to go in, and the time is good because there's nothing else in the room.

If, however, you must make choices based on limited resources, prioritize what you need to make the room look and feel functional and to be happy in it. Make those choices in the context of the whole project. Decide what is first needed to make the room or home useable, and then determine whether a large chunk of your budget is best spent on one aspect.

As you consider the function of the room, get input from the entire family. What will they be using this room

Love the space you're in.

for? If it's a family room, look at the size and ask, "Is seating for watching television a primary function? For how many? Do you want multiple seating areas so that people can read, work on the computer, play games, or sit and have conversations? If you will be socializing more here, how many people will need to be accommodated?" These considerations are similar for a dining room. How many people will be in the dining room?

Many dining rooms are too small for the groups that use them, or their layout is not practical.

One of the things I've always fantasized about doing is to strategically position all of my furniture and then build the walls around it so that I truly have the optimal space I want. This is beginning with the end in mind. If you are in a position to build a house, my challenge to you is to take this perspective.

Most of us own the kind of house that we have in order to fit whatever we want within its confines.

Most of us own the kind of house that we have in order to fit whatever we want within its confines.

Look at what exists and ask what the function is going to be: is it a dining room, a kitchen, a family room, a bedroom? Bedrooms, for example, come in a variety of sizes. If it's the master bedroom suite, ask yourself if you want an exercise area that's separate or a part of the room. Do you want a desk? What about a TV or an armoire? What's the closet situation? Is a closet attached to the bathroom? Is there a linen closet or storage space? These are all considerations or conditions of satisfaction with respect to how the space will function for you.

DESIGNING AROUND ROOM COMPONENTS

As you prepare to design your room, note its components, its unique features. Review the windows; other architectural features such as built-in cabinetry or moldings; and the material of the walls, floors, and ceiling.

In the column titled "What's Working?" on Worksheet #2 "Evaluate Your Space" (see Appendix), list the characteristics of each line item in detail. As an example, for floors, identify whether you have hardwood, carpet, tile, combination, or other. Also identify the color and any pattern or texture. If what exists must be replaced, list what needs to be replaced in the "What Needs Replacing?" column, and indicate what it will be replaced with if you have an idea. If you do not have an idea yet, list the change as TBD and highlight it for further thought.

As you go through the detail of the evaluation worksheet, you have the opportunity to understand the many parts that make up the decor of your room. It is important to evaluate each part and determine how it fits in with your personal style. Take, for example, paneling in a room. It has a color. It has texture. It's associated with a particular style of decorating. Whether you like it or you don't depends on how you feel about paneling in general and whether it's your style or not. Some people just love the wood grain, and they treat it with a clear stain, a natural wood stain, or a color. If you don't like the wood look, painting it may be the best thing to do. Other options are to wallpaper over it or take it down.

Photo courtesy of Janet Aurora, Styleprint Designer, Hambley Team

Walls make up a major portion of the decor in the room. They are the largest space, and their visual presence is at eye level, and yet they are considered to be part of the "foundation" of the room because they are "behind the scenes." What that means is that they are the backdrop for everything else. Furnishings, window treatments, artwork, and even many lighting fixtures will be viewed "on top of" the walls. As you are evaluating the walls, consider putting them into the context of a supporting role and not the lead in the cast.

Within this context, consider all of the different types of materials used for walls: drywall, plaster, paneling, stucco, tile, logs, glass, stone, brick, and upholstered, to name a few. Also consider the condition of the walls. Are they in need of repair, cleaning, or simply some cosmetic enhancements? As the homeowner, you could complete some repairs yourself. Others may require the expertise of a professional.

The walls and floors account for 60 percent of your decor. Keep this in mind as you allocate color, pattern, and texture. Whatever you choose to do here will have a huge impact on the final result of your room and how well it accomplishes your desired result.

In some rooms, particularly kitchens and bathrooms, there are additional surface finishes that will add to your personal decor style. Granite counter-tops are more prevalent than they were 30 years ago since their cost has decreased. Laminates, which are least expensive, are another option, and then there are materials such as Caesarstone, Corian, marble, tile, and natural wood.

THE STYLEPRINT® DESIGN SYSTEM TECHNICAL DÉCOR INFO: KITCHEN COUNTERTOP SURFACES

MATERIAL	DESCRIPTION
Bamboo	Sustainable, natural material; not high durability—water can warp.
Butcher Block	Laminated wood; needs sealing for moisture resistance; knife marks create character—or sanding can eliminate/reduce.
Glass	Sleek; tempered glass = clear or translucent w/smooth or textured surface; waterproof and heat tolerant; will scratch.
Granite	Natural stone; has a particular look; durable and impervious to heat; requires professional installation and periodic sealing.
Laminate	Engineered plywood/durable nonporous surface material with a thin veneer as a top layer with choice of hundreds of colors/patterns as faux stone, marble, etc. Affordable material, easy to install. may scratch—use a cutting board.
Marble and Limestone	Natural stone; more porous and softer than granite which makes them likely to scratch or stain; recommend periodic sealing treatment; cultured marble: made from natural marble chips embedded in plastic resin; comes in sheets, more economical and can be used in the bathroom for countertops and walls.
Quartz-Surfacing	A.k.a. engineered stone; blend of quartz, resins, and pigments, which will produce a consistent stone like pattern; non-porous and heat/scratch resistant.

Soapstone	Natural stone; resists heat; chips more easily than granite; treat with mineral oil to repel moisture and maintain its classic look.
Solid-Surfacing	One version is Corian™; alternate is a plastic resin available in many colors and patterns; non-porous; stain resistant; resists scratches (can be sanded out); a sink can be made seamless—easier installation.
Stainless Steel	Sanitary, stain proof, heatproof, waterproof, shiny finish may show scratches and fingerprints.
Tile	Glazed ceramic or porcelain come in many sizes, shapes, colors; water and heat resistant; may chip; variety of price points; requires grout; tiles are easy care; grout may stain and require cleaning or regrouting periodically.

The primary consideration with all of the finishes is that your choices coordinate and blend well together. No choice is isolated. This is especially true when it comes to color. Everything has a color. You either start with a finish that you love and build the rest of the room around it, or you find a finish that complements the room.

For a room to be considered "well designed," everything in the room—all the colors, patterns, and textures—must flow together.

In addition—and this is critical—think about the care and maintenance of the items you choose. Check with the professional you are purchasing the product from to find out how durable it is and what kind of care it needs. Will you have to treat the item once a month? Once a year? Never? How do you clean it? How do you maintain it? What if something spills on it? Does it scratch easily? It's important to learn about the care that will be required and to select materials that match your level of willingness to care for them and will be durable, depending on how you use them—much like clothing. Can the product be washed, or must it be dry-cleaned? Is that something you are okay with, or will you be annoyed and irritated every time you have to take care of it? This will also be important with respect to the resale value of your home. Whatever you choose must wear well so that at the time of sale it's not looking shabby and worn. Additionally, how will a potential buyer react to the level of care required?

DECORATING FEAR FACTORS: TURN THEM INTO REASONS FOR TAKING ACTION

If you're starting or contemplating a decorating project, you're bound to run into a few fears and limitations that may cause you to get stuck. Here are four great ways to stay motivated and moving ahead:

1. Enjoy the process of the project.

2. Stick to your plan, and avoid project creep.

3. Set a realistic time frame to complete it.

4. Check your progress along the way.

TV decorating shows are good news and bad news for your confidence in home decor improvement. First, the good news: they are inspiring. Wow! Look what can be done! The bad news: the results the show gets are not nearly as simple, easy, and inexpensive as the producers would like you to think. Consider that they have an untold number of talented and experienced craftspeople working as a team. They have sponsors who donate materials and time. Their mission is to get your attention, and what they do might not necessarily have the same effect on your space. We have also seen shows in which the owners end up underwhelmed because the decorators, wanting to surprise the owners, come up with a look without involving them. The result reflects someone else's style and not the preferences and taste of the homeowners.

What are the most common fears that people have about decorating projects? From my 30-plus years of experience in working with clients and coaching other DecorDesigners to work with clients, here are the top nine. Do any of these apply to you?

1. How do I select and use color for maximum effect and enjoyment?

2. Will it cost more than I planned to invest?

3. Will it take longer to complete than I want?

4. Will it be of a quality that is healthy for the inhabitants and last for the time I want?

5. What safety concerns do I need to be aware of?

6. Will it be easy to maintain?

7. Will the space function as I want and need it to?

8. Will it be comfortable?

9. The ultimate question is will it make me smile and feel pleased with the results?

If any of these apply to you, you are not alone. The purpose of this book—and the Styleprint Design System—is to take the fear out of your decorating projects, get at least one into motion, and enjoy the results.

#1 COLOR: HOW DO I SELECT AND USE COLOR FOR MAXIMUM EFFECT AND ENJOYMENT?

The fear of using color can stop some people in their tracks. They worry about which color to choose … whether it should be light/dark/warm/cool … where to use it … how to use it … how it will look … whether they'll get tired of it … how it blends with other colors … where to start and stop … and on and on.

Solution: If you want to do some preliminary research, go to a paint store or the paint section of a home improvement store. These stores often have tear sheets or brochures of current color trends and combinations. In addition, they usually have photos of those colors in room settings to help you visualize. All of this will assist in narrowing down your color preferences. One word of caution: be open to colors that you may not have considered previously. There are over 16 million colors available. Do not limit yourself just because you have never used a color before.

Here are some recommended websites with information on color and color selection:

- www.sensationalcolor.com

- www.behr.com

- www.sherwin-williams.com

- www.benjaminmoore.com

We address many of these nine questions later in the book, but color is one of the areas where a professional can step in and really help. The reason is twofold. First, a professional has been trained in color and how to use it. Second, a professional can serve as an objective eye in the project, asking and answering questions from an unbiased perspective.

What people are really afraid of is taking a risk or making a blunder, so that, sometimes, they never get going at all.

#2 INVESTMENT: WILL IT COST MORE THAN I PLANNED TO INVEST?

Whether the project stays within budget will depend on how thoroughly you've thought it through. If you have done your research on what things cost, requested quotes from contractors, and truly nailed the scope of the project, you can expect to be within a realistic range. When it comes to implementing projects and keeping the dollars in alignment with your intention, it all comes back to your focus:

What people are really afraid of is taking a risk or making a blunder, so that, sometimes, they never get going at all.

understanding what is involved so that you can select what you want within your dollar range and not get carried away with add-ons. It's similar to building a house or buying a new car: Starting with the basics, it's easy to upgrade in small amounts that add up quickly so that you can easily exceed what you intended to spend.

Solution: Plan your project, know your parameters, and do your research so that you have a realistic investment range to work with.

#3 TIME: WILL IT TAKE LONGER TO COMPLETE THAN I WANT?

People worry about how much time the project is going to take. It's important to allow time for planning, for thinking through the project, for saying, "What is it that I really want this room to do for me? How will we use the room? How will it function? How will it feel? How will it look?" It's also important to understand the time it takes to complete the different aspects of the project. Will you need a painter? How long will it take to get on his/her schedule? How long will that piece of the project take? If you intend to do the painting yourself, how much time do you have to devote to it? Look at your calendar. Schedule the project with some buffer time. Look at the sequencing of things that need to happen to complete the project and schedule that out.

Solution: Think ahead and plan. Refer to the worksheets that accompany this book. Take the time to complete Worksheet #1 ("Focus Step") and Worksheet #2 ("Evaluate Your Space.") You may find some subtle aspects that are more important than you thought. You may also find some hidden to-dos that will eat up some time. Through planning and being realistic about how fast all the parts can be completed, you will have a better sense of how long the project will take. Be sure to build in some additional time to handle things that don't go as smoothly as planned.

#4 QUALITY: WILL IT BE OF A QUALITY THAT IS HEALTHY FOR THE INHABITANTS AND LAST FOR THE TIME I WANT?

Quality is another area where people are afraid to make a mistake. There are many different levels of quality for every type of product in a decor plan. You may not want heirloom quality for your furnishings— something that you want to pass down from generation to generation. You also may not want "curbside" quality. Curbside quality is made of inferior materials, often has harmful chemicals used in its production, and, typically, has a short life because it's not well made. Ultimately, curbside furniture ends up being thrown out long before you are ready to replace it.

Solution: Select the level of quality that's appropriate with respect to your dollar investment, the longevity/durability you desire, and the healthful aspect of its production.

#5 SAFETY: WHAT SAFETY CONCERNS DO I NEED TO BE AWARE OF?

Safety is sometimes taken for granted but is of concern to many people. The materials in furnishings can be toxic—for instance, they may contain formaldehyde or other chemicals that people are sensitive to and can even make them sick. Alternately, some products have a dangerous design. For example, the cords on some window blinds are hazardous, even lethal, to pets and children. Some reputable manufacturers have designed alternative lift systems for these shades or have crafted the cording so that it breaks away when weight is applied to it so that nothing, child or pet, gets caught in it.

Solution: Ask questions about the product, what it's made of, how it traveled to where it's sold, and what its safety features are.

#6 MAINTENANCE: WILL IT BE EASY TO MAINTAIN?

Concern about maintenance does not always surface at the beginning of a project, but it certainly becomes a factor once you're living with it. After all, we don't actually live in "look at," magazine-type rooms.

Solution: Think about maintenance early on, and make it a part of your plan. The furnishings and materials available today have many features that help you keep them looking good despite people living on and with them.

Photo courtesy of Kelly Murphy, Styleprint Designer

#7 AND #8 PLANNING: WILL THE SPACE BE COMFORTABLE AND FUNCTION AS I WANT AND NEED IT TO?

The answers to these questions depend on your planning. When you prepared Worksheet #1 ("Focus Step"), were you thorough? Did you delineate these concerns? And when you prepared Worksheet #2

("Evaluate Your Space"), did you list these requirements in the columns titled, "What is to be added?" or "What is to be replaced?"

Solution: Take a few minutes to go back and review these worksheets and make any changes that will be important to the success of your project.

One important thing to note here: if you choose to work with professionals, an added benefit is that you also have the opportunity to bounce ideas off them. You might say, "This might be a wild idea, but ..." or "Gee, I've often wondered what if we paint only one wall? How would that work? Is that a totally crazy idea or not?" The professional might respond by asking other questions to determine if the idea is valid, and if it doesn't have merit, discussing why not. In the end you will have the satisfaction of knowing that all options were considered. This will contribute to your confidence in the direction selected.

#9 UNDERLYING DRIVE: WILL I REALLY LIKE IT WHEN IT IS FINISHED? WILL IT MAKE ME SMILE, AND WILL I BE PLEASED WITH THE RESULTS?

These fears are high on your list because you want the results to reflect the time and resources that you invest. It's your home, and you want it to look, feel, and function based on your personal preferences, not someone else's. And you don't want the result to miss the mark.

Photo courtesy of Dana Petrie, Styleprint Designer

Solution: You must take the time to ask yourself questions about your preferences and focus for the room, and you must think about your room in detail. If you are not clear on what you want, your result will be mediocre at best. How could it be any different? It takes time to carefully plan for what you want and to think things through.

Let's recap Styleprint discovery. This chapter is about:

1. Thinking about your space and imagining what you would like it to be

2. Analyzing your space (what works vs. what doesn't) from three perspectives:

   ☐ its intended function

   ☐ its physical characteristics

   ☐ your personal preferences

3. Evaluating principles of good design:

   ☐ light

   ☐ color

   ☐ arrangement within the walls

   ☐ the details

4. Evaluating options with respect to

   ☐ investment

   ☐ complexity

5. Being aware of fear factors and their impact on the project:

   ☐ creating a plan

   ☐ implementing the plan

In the next chapter, we will take the next step: following through on your project to select the items and their specifications to meet your personal preferences and expectations of good design and prioritizing those items with respect to what you are willing to do, the level of investment, the order in which to do them, and a targeted timeline.

CHAPTER TWO

STEP 2: THE STYLE SUCCESS SURVEY

Ideally, the impact we are going for here is to direct your thinking about your space and how to decorate it for personal satisfaction and enjoyment. Ultimately, it's about choices and ensuring that those choices produce the look, feel, and function that you desire for your space.

The Style Success Survey is the step in your journey where you clarify the scope of the project. Is it an entire room or home, or is it a part? In Worksheet #2 ("Evaluate Your Space"), you highlighted all the things that could be done by either adding or replacing items. You must now determine what you are willing to do, all from the perspective that you identified on your "Focus Step" Worksheet #1:

- How many items will you add or replace?

- What is the budget range for this project at this time?

- What might you defer to a later time?

- Where will you begin? What makes the most sense?

Worksheet #3, "Your Styleprint Specifics" (see Appendix), reviews the entire room (or entire home), item by item, with respect to the scope of your project. You identify what you are willing to change or add. In this chapter and the next, you identify the possibilities available to you and make selections. First, you identify what the options are. Second, you eliminate the options that are beyond what you are willing to commit to or are not in line with your personal preferences.

In order to make the best choices for your room design, we will consider:

- lighting

- the color plan

- walls, floors, and ceilings

- furnishings

- storage

- windows

- art and accessories

- greenery

FINDING A STARTING POINT

You have to limit your choices at some point, or you won't ever do anything. All you have to do is pick a spot and begin.

THE WHEEL OF DECORATING

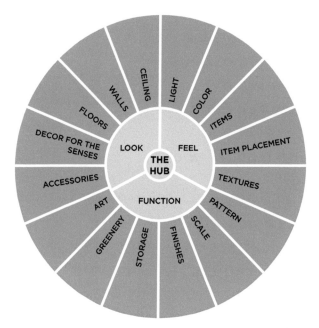

INSTRUCTIONS:
Assess the space for all of the parts.
Draw it out. Collect the samples/
photos. Plan the details.

WHERE TO BEGIN?

It's simply a matter of selecting a direction. And just because we're going in one particular direction doesn't mean there won't be many choices within that direction. Pick a place, and we'll get started creating your space for enjoyment, something that you're happy with. Then we'll show you how to pull the ribbon of that creation around the rest of the house so that it's all coordinated and tied together.

When people ask what room to begin decorating in, I usually ask them, "Where do you spend most of your time?"

Each choice will have an effect on all other choices

When people ask what room to begin decorating in, I usually ask them, "Where do you spend most of your time?"

First, determine your starting point. Is it a room that you want to decorate, or is it a category that you want to approach first? For example, if you decided to replace the windows in your home, you will want to review your window coverings, or if you are replacing flooring in more than one room, you will want to address that first. Anywhere you decide to start, the critical thing to remember is that each choice is not totally independent, just the opposite. Each choice will have an effect on all other choices—new choices must be blended into the mix of past choices and will also affect the direction of future selections.

BUDGETING IS THE PIVOTAL POINT (ALLOCATION OF FINANCIAL RESOURCES)

What and how much you do is a function of the financial resources and level of complexity that the project encompasses. If there aren't enough resources to implement a plan, then we're just having a conversation, and the plan will be nothing more than a good idea. Between your "Focus" worksheet and your "Evaluation" worksheet you now have an idea of your commitment and financial parameters. So the conversation becomes, "What are your priorities for decorating? If you could make an impact on your highest priority first, what would you like to see happen there? Do you feel a total redo is needed, or do you think we can spruce it up? Can we use some of your furnishings and add to that?"

Next, research and review the price range(s) for what you want replaced or added. Consider what else might be needed and allocate dollars for that. Also, consider an alternative approach. How else can you accomplish the same thing? Add up the price ranges and determine what is doable and what is not, or do the project in stages: complete one part now and tackle the next in six months.

SAMPLE BUDGET FOR HOME DECOR PROJECT

ROOM	ITEMS	INVESTMENT RANGES			
		AMBIANCE	CASUAL ELEGANCE	LUXURY	LUXURY PLUS
Living Room/Family Room	Seating for 6 (sofa/loveseat/chairs)	$7,000	$10,000	$15,000	
	Additional seating per seat	$1,400	$2,800	$6,000	
	Ottoman	$1,000	$2,000	$3,000	
	End Tables, Cocktail Table, Sofa Table	$2,000	$4,000	$6,000	
	Window Treatments (Fabric) 3-36" windows	$1,200	$2,400	$4,800	
	Window Treatments (Privacy/Light Control)	$500	$1,500	$4,500	
	Area Rug (8x10)	$1,400	$3,000	$5,000	
	Lighting (3 Lamps)	$1,000	$2,000	$2,500	
	Accessories	$1,000	$4,000	$6,000	
	Wallcovering (room 15' x 22')	$1,250	$1,800	$2,500	
	Flooring (room 15' x 22') carpet	$1,500	$2,100	$3,200	
	Flooring (room 15' x 22') hardwood	$3,750	$4,500	$5,500	
	other				
	TOTAL:				
Dining Room	Table for 8	$2,000	$4,000	$6,000	
	6 side chairs; 2 host/hostess	$5,000	$7,500	$9,000	
	Window Treatments (Fabric) 3-36" windows	$1,200	$2,400	$4,800	
	Window Treatments (Privacy/Light Control)	$500	$1,500	$4,500	
	Area Rug (8x10)	$1,400	$3,000	$5,000	
	Chandelier/Overhead Lighting, 2 lamps	$2,000	$4,000	$6,000	
	Server	$2,000	$4,000	$6,000	
	Accessories	$1,000	$4,000	$6,000	
	Wallcovering (room 12' x 18')	$1,100	$1,650	$2,300	

	Flooring (room 12' x 18') carpet	$1,200	$1,700	$2,300
	Flooring (room 12' x 18') hardwood	$2,500	$3,200	$4,000
	other:			
	TOTAL:			
Bedroom	Queen Bed	$2,500	$4,000	$6,000
	Queen Bedding	$2,000	$3,000	$5,000
	Night Stands	$1,000	$2,000	$4,000
	Window Treatments (Fabric) 3-36" windows	$1,200	$2,400	$4,800
	Window Treatments (Fabric) Top treatments	$1,200	$2,400	$4,800
	Window Treatments (Privacy/Light Control)	$500	$1,500	$4,500
	Area Rug (8x10)	$1,400	$3,000	$5,000
	Lighting (3 Lamps)	$1,000	$2,000	$2,500
	Accessories	$1,000	$4,000	$6,000
	Seating for 2	$3,000	$5,000	$7,000
	Wallcovering (room 12' x 18')	$1,100	$1,650	$2,300
	Flooring (room 12' x 18') carpet	$1,200	$1,700	$2,300
	Flooring (room 12' x 18') hardwood	$2,500	$3,200	$4,000
	other:			
	TOTAL:			

* Note: These are guesstimates for $$ to invest in a Decor Project to help you define your project.

The actual $$ will vary regionally and by the options selected.

The $$ include a quality, professional installation by a reputable company. Warranties of product have disclaimer clauses for poor installation.

The investment ranges have purposely NOT included the lowest investments available.

A Better Business Bureau fact: 80% of the complaints in the home improvement industry come from consumers who selected the lowest bid.

Determine what items are a priority and which items exist that you will keep.

Luxury Plus is at your discretion—higher investments can always be made.

Decorating can run from A to Z in terms of investment. Remember your home is your sanctuary; plan to maximize the dollars you put into it so that you get high value back in terms of function and enjoyment. That may mean splurging on the investment—within reason.

Some rooms and homes are not a blank canvas. They may be completely decorated but outdated. What happens then? Do you throw out everything and start over? Or do you work with what you have? You will determine this. What do you want to do? Look at everything critically. What are the pieces that you absolutely love and don't want to get rid of? What are the pieces that you don't love but, for whatever reason, you have to keep? They could be family heirlooms or something sentimental.

Ultimately, it all goes back to the resources. How many dollars are you allocating to this? How much time? Do you have enough to start from scratch—a blank canvas?

When it comes to a budget, we all have a fantasy number in our mind. A fantasy number is the dollar amount that you would like to spend on the project. Many times, this is an unrealistic number. Nevertheless, if we can get it done for that, that would be great!

Ultimately, you will have a hard and fast dollar range you must stick to.

If you're doing this for yourself, you have to play two roles. You have to step outside yourself at given points and not look at things in terms of what you *like* but in light of the *function*, the *feel*, and the *look* that you're going for. There is no one right way to do it. There are always going to be other options, other roads not taken, but you don't want to make a lifelong pursuit out of decorating this room. Instead, ask yourself what your best options are right now—the ones that are easily accessible to you—so that you can transform this room and get on with the rest of your life.

When it comes to a budget, we all have a fantasy number in our mind. A fantasy number is the dollar amount that you would like to spend on the project. Many times, this is an unrealistic number. Nevertheless, if we can get it done for that, that would be great! Ultimately, you will have a hard and fast dollar range you must stick to.

Side note: There is a point where having a professional to work with you, someone who brings a trained, objective eye, can be invaluable. That expert may be able to help you sort through your stuff and recommend a good direction for you to take.

SIZING UP THE SPACE

Once you have decided on a direction, it's time to get to the hands-on part. Measure, take photographs, lay out your furnishings on graph paper on a scale of one-quarter inch for every foot, use an app such as Google Sketchup, or go to the Better Homes and Gardens website: http://arrangearoom.bhg.com. Keep functionality as your number-one focus here. Do three of these layouts, and evaluate the success of each. Is anything missing? Does it all fit? How about the color scheme? Is that coming together so that you can visualize it and feel good about it? Be open to putting something in your plan that you may not have originally thought of. As you work this through, new ideas and thoughts will pop into your mind. Write them down for later consideration. Don't dismiss them immediately.

Having choices is important, as it helps to ensure that your final selections are what you want. Even if you do not think an arrangement is something you will like, that's okay. Think it through anyway so that you can look at it and say, "No, I really don't like that."

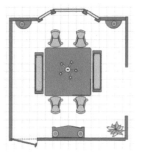 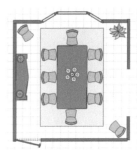

Sometimes, in completing this exercise, you will find that a layout you were considering doesn't work. There may not be enough room to fit all the furnishings with enough clearance to easily walk around. A small guest room may have a queen-size bed. In that case, one option is to push the bed up against the wall, but that causes problems with access when two people are sleeping in the bed. It's also difficult to change the sheets and make the bed. It can be done, but it's not the best arrangement.

Humans are very much creatures of comfort, ease, and convenience. We tend to slide over things or not do some things if they seem inconvenient. So make your space as comfortable and convenient as possible, whether it's for watching TV, reading, doing homework, playing games, exercising, or cooking; the space is best utilized when it flows easily.

CRITICAL TO SUCCESS: ROOM ARRANGEMENT

Begin by drawing your plan on *paper*. Even though you can find room arrangement apps online, the brain works differently when your fingers are writing or drawing on paper than when you are using a digital device. It's much like learning math. First, you use pencil and paper. Once you grasp the concept, a calculator becomes a useful tool.

Better yet, use graph paper for your room arrangements, with a quarter inch equaling a foot. We have included a couple blank sheets of graph paper in the appendix and on our website: www.styleprintdesignsystem.com.

Do your layout to scale so that you'll be able to see pieces of furniture in relation to everything else. How wide, for example, is the sofa? All sofas are not equal. Accurate measurements are important in deciding whether or not your sofa will fit in a particular space. If it's a piece you already have and are keeping, those measurements will enable you to incorporate it in the room. If it's an item you must purchase, you will need to know the particulars when shopping.

THE STYLEPRINT DESIGN SYSTEM TECHNICAL DECOR INFO: TRAFFIC PLANNING GUIDELINES

Major walkway	4'-5' wide
Subsidiary route	27"-3' wide
Between sofa/cocktail table	18"-24" max
Between sofa/end table	3"-5"
Conversational grouping	8' max
DINING ROOM	
Between chairs	18"
Chairs	2' for pulling chair back; 3' total from edge of table
Area rug	Accommodate table and 3' beyond to accommodate people and chair.
Between table and wall	4'
BEDROOM	
In front of dresser	3' to allow for ease of getting in and out of drawers
Wall and bed	18" min
Night table height	Equal to mattress height
Dresser height	No lower than mattress height
Lamps	No higher than headboard
OTHER DETAILS	
End table height	Equal to height of sofa arm
Cocktail table height	Equal to seat height of chair/ sofa
Sofa/console tables	Equal to sofa back height
TV	Best viewing is directly in front of; distance depends on TV size; check for light reflections/glare

Other important aspects of functional space are walkways, conversational groupings of furnishings, and the distance from the TV. The optimal distance between a sofa and coffee table is, typically, 18 inches. This will allow someone to move in and around them. That amount of space between a dining room table and a sideboard or buffet table is not enough. There, you need three feet to get in and out of a chair.

A walkway, generally, is about two feet wide; a major area walkway is three to four feet wide. In a family room where there is a grouping of furniture, such as a sofa and a couple of chairs, check to make sure there is a way for people to get in, get out, and move around easily. Curved pathways (versus angular) make it easier for people to move around. Consider details of function when planning a room. A room that does not allow for function and movement with ease is not a well-designed room and, ultimately, will be subconsciously avoided.

If you have children, it's best not to block a walkway with furniture, because children will tend to jump over the furniture rather than walk around it.

Sketch out your room quickly on plain paper. Next, using graph paper, draw it to scale. Look for traffic patterns and consider the width of walkways.

Make three room arrangements, and then make your selection. To get the feeling of the three-dimensional space, move whatever pieces you already have into the space where you want them, and use boxes as placeholders for the furniture you plan to buy.

Don't start moving furniture before making a plan. It's better to draw it, review it, and move things around on paper. That way, you can get a feel for what will work best, not just what you like visually. It's easier on your back as well.

If you have children, it's best not to block a walkway with furniture, because children will tend to jump over the furniture rather than walk around it.

If you are moving, start by planning out one room, and then complete all rooms prior to the move. Knowing where you want items placed will make moving day so much easier compared to planning on the fly and deciding where to put each item as it comes off the truck, putting it there, and later, reconsidering and moving it again. That adds tons of extra work to an already exhausting day. Be smart and plan it out first.

If you are moving and having to downsize, it's imperative that you measure out the space, identify the pieces of furniture you want to bring (checking that the sizes work in the new space), and identify the new things you want. Beginning with the result in mind, taking the steps to plan accordingly will, ultimately, eliminate much unnecessary frustration. You will be able to move in, get settled, and relax quickly.

In addition to determining whether a piece will fit in the room sizewise, its comfort must also be considered. Comfort is derived from four things: (1) personal preference (for example, whether you like cushions to be cushy, firm, or in between), (2) whether the seating is designed for the user's body type (for example, seat depth will vary with the height of the user), (3) the scale of the piece in relation to the size of the room (for example, oversized pieces will look out of place in a small room), and (4) the construction of the piece. All of this is factored into the design and product selection for the room. Pieces must not only fit, be appropriate in scale, and be well coordinated, they must also meet the criteria of those living there.

THE STYLEPRINT® DESIGN SYSTEM
TECHNICAL DÉCOR INFO: FURNITURE

SOFA, a basic range of measurements (custom and non-typical sizing can be found):

Outside dimensions:

Width	80, 84, 86, 88, 90, 94
Depths	36, 38, 40, 42, 44
Back height	30, 37, 39
Seat depth	22
Seat Height	18, 20, 22
Arm height	24, 26

LOVESEAT

Width	46, 56, 60, 65, 72

All other dimensions same as above

UPHOLSTERED CHAIRS:

Width	34, 36, 40, 42

CUSHION TYPES:

Foam—varying densities

Foam core (varying densities) with wrap of poly-fiber or down

Down-all down (different types of down)

Down wrapped

Springs—wrapped in poly-fiber or down

BASIC CONSTRUCTIONS:

Sinuous Spring construction: refers to the seat structure; has a sinuous seat system using

S-shaped springs tied together with steel wire ensuring a consistent seating platform; Over wood or wood composite frames with rolled edges, high quality decking and padding; joints reinforced with corner braces screwed and glued for added strength.

Eight-Way Hand Tied construction: (historically considered to be the gold standard in the industry): refers to seat structure; has a premium quality 8-way hand-tied coil system using tempered steel coil springs tied at 8 points for comfort and proper seat support; steel bands under each row of springs reinforce the construction for lasting comfort; over kiln-dried hardwood or wood composite with rolled edges, high quality decking and padding; joints secured and reinforced with corner braces glued and screwed for added strength and comfort.

PLACING FURNITURE IN A ROOM PLAN

When planning a room, select the scale of furnishings that will enhance the room. If it's a smaller room and you want it to look and feel bigger, go with lighter colors because lighter colors open up space and make walls recede. Look for other ways to add light to the room since light creates the illusion that the room is bigger. (Conversely, less light pulls the room in and makes it feel cozier.) In addition, do not select overstuffed upholstered pieces, massive-size furnishings, or extra-large tables.

Photo courtesy of Karen Powell, Styleprint Creator and Designer

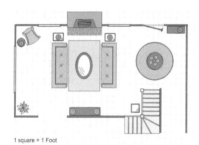

1 square = 1 Foot

Good design calls for an environment that supports the lifestyle of those living in it and gives them pleasure.

This is not a book about decorating living spaces for display in a glossy magazine; you want to smile and feel comfortable every time you look at your space.

Decorate for those who will be living in the space. This doesn't mean it has to look shabby or unfinished. It can look as elegant as you want as long as it's livable without constant fuss. It has to support the people who inhabit the space.

Good design calls for an environment that supports the lifestyle of those living in it and gives them pleasure.

Reminder: your challenge is to be open to possibilities you might not have considered. Create one plan that is outrageously different from what you would usually go for. Ultimately, you're going to select the one that you want, so dream a little!

THE IMPORTANCE OF STORAGE

Historically, there was a time when storage was a critical feature in a house. I think we've backed off from that a bit. It's still important, and certainly, when you're buying a house, you want to be sure there's adequate closet space for clothing and other possessions. However, you can go too far in that direction. I did this in my own family room when I decided I wanted a storage ottoman instead of a coffee table. I thought it would be a great idea, and it was a great idea. It stored a lot of stuff that, once it got in there, I never looked at again. So when I redid my family room, I said, "Out with this. It's too much storage because I'm not using what is in it."

My advice is to think about what you really need to store. Do you really want to store it and give up all that valuable space, or do you want something different that will support your life better? Think about where you can put things and how many things you really want to keep. Be thoughtful about that, and don't go crazy with too much storage. Sometimes, we are just hesitant to retire some possessions.

Photo courtesy of Janet Aurora, Styleprint Designer, Hambley Team

Back to our example: I found a different type of cocktail table for my family room. It had a glass top and a glass shelf underneath where I put magazines and books. Everyone could see them there, and they were not in the way. Then I placed a beautiful, contemporary candelabra on the table, which made a nice centerpiece. I could put a drinking glass on the table without all the clutter in the way.

The Style Success Survey is encompassed in Worksheet #2, "Evaluate Your Space," and in Worksheet #3, "Your Styleprint Specifics," in the Appendix and online at www.styleprintdesignsystem. com. These worksheets detail the choices you have started to consider.

CHAPTER THREE

STEP 3: CREATING YOUR POSSIBILITIES

It is necessary to take two concurrent paths to create and complete the room, home, or office that will make you want to say, "Wow! I love my space. It's everything that I need and want!" The first path is the logistics sequence. This is where you identify the result you want and consider the options for achieving it. In the first two chapters, we considered the thought and planning needed to achieve the result you desire. The second path is good design according to accepted industry standards. This chapter focuses on creating your best result by identifying the "whats" that are required to accomplish that result. This is where you drill down into the design elements, guided by your personal preferences.

As you move through this chapter, create three unique plans—three possibilities—for consideration. It's always nice to say no to something because it validates the things you say yes to, resulting in less buyer's remorse or thinking, *I should have …* And do not just select the same old things that you always gravitate toward. Have at least one plan that is out of character for you. This is a great exercise to stretch your thinking a bit, and sometimes you will find something that is more enticing than you expected when it is paired with other things you are more comfortable with. Remember you do not have to choose it. You are just thinking about options at this time.

A plan consists of all the components that will be needed to create your WOW room:

- a lighting plan

- a color theme/plan

- a room arrangement layout drawn to scale

- photos/swatches of all items to put in the room

- the financial investment required for the plan

- the time frame estimated to complete the plan

- a list of behind the scenes you will need to do to facilitate the completion of the plan

(i.e. donate a used piece of furniture, clean out the chest, etc.)

See sample: Your Styleprint plan. Also available on the website: www.styleprintdesignsystem.com.

YOUR STYLEPRINT PLAN

POWERPOINT TEMPLATE

Create a powerpoint presentation for your Styleprint Plan. Create one to two slides per section:

Room: _____

Plan #: _____

Drop in photo(s)

Descriptors:

1.

2.

3.

Lighting plan

Drop in photos of fixtures

Color theme

Dominant color
placement   %

Secondary color
placement   %

Accent color
placement   %

Medium: Paint

Wallcovering

Furnishings:

Existing furnishings (drop in photos)

Additional furnishings (drop in photos of samples)

Window treatments (drop in sketches and fabric)

Art (drop in selected pieces)

Greenery (drop in selections)

Accessories/Other items (drop in photos of samples)

Other (drop in photos of samples)

Senses side of your décor:

Visual is all of the above.

Touch: what textures are used and where?

Auditory:

Scent:

Taste:

Investment range:

By category:

Time frame estimate:

As an example, I have helped many clients choose sofas with fabric colors that blend with the colors of their pets. This is not a direction they would have originally chosen. You might relate to this. If the pet is allowed on the sofa, do not think that just because you are getting a new sofa, the pet will no longer be allowed on it. If the dog is a member of the family and has sofa rights, don't fight it. I don't suggest buying a new sofa that will look bad if the pet sheds. It's going to look ugly all the time. Work with it! Think about it and smile. You will appreciate it.

SEEING THE BIG PICTURE

The key to good design is to look at your space differently than you've ever looked at it before. You want to think about things that you might have written off—"Oh no, I'm not going to do that." At least consider alternatives. You don't have to do them, but at least consider them. If you love your home, then any dollars that you put into that space are going to give you enjoyment. Why not enjoy it even more than you did before?

Pick two to three things to put in the room that you love; everything else builds on and complements those items. If you feel that you have to love everything in the room, you will end up frustrated. It won't make sense, it won't function or look or feel good, and it won't accomplish your goal of absolutely loving the room.

Pick two or three things that you love, and everything else will build around them.

It all comes back to evaluating the space to find what's working and what's not—for the look, feel, and function that people want.

This is where decorating is counterintuitive. If you love everything, your eye doesn't know where to settle. It jumps between all of the things that you love. You are much better advised to pick two to three things that you love and have the rest of the room support them. This is an important concept for people who are decorating on their own for the first time. Usually, this is a big aha moment. It's counterintuitive; it does not seem logical.

It all comes back to evaluating the space to find what's working and what's not—for the look, feel, and function that people want.

A NOTE ABOUT THE
IMPORTANCE OF STYLE

The 1970s and early 1980s boasted particular decorating styles, be they traditional, contemporary, or country. In the late 1980s and 1990s, home inhabitants morphed styles to be less strict, with greater blurring of the lines between them. Style became "personal" or "eclectic" and later, "transitional." This mind-set continues in decorating today; people decorate in a much more eclectic style. They combine things that are pleasing, comfortable, and practical for them.

Personal style boils down to what you like. If you like detail, you might want a camelback sofa with carved-wood legs or items that are a bit more on the traditional side. If you like sleeker, cleaner lines, you will lean toward contemporary style, which has less intricate detail. Your style tendencies will have an impact on what you ultimately select and reject for your decor.

If you are into classic design and like tailored lines that are crisp, clean, and neat, consider a sofa cushion that is formed, boxlike. It can have a shape to it and still be comfy and soft. If you like things tailored, you don't want to continually fluff up cushions, but if you like things a little more free flowing, with more of a rumpled, "shabby chic" look, down cushions will be more your style. Match yourself to a decor style that really suits your tastes and your lifestyle.

Most of the time, it's pretty clear what you like. It will come out in different ways. First, it comes out in what you don't want. A good exercise is to look through decorating magazines or HOUZZ online and tag things that you like and don't like. You can learn as much from the things you don't like as you can from the things that you gravitate toward. It's also important to keep your hobbies, interests, and favorite travel spots in mind as you consider your decor plans because they often provide a starting point.

Photo courtesy of Karen Powell, Styleprint Creator and Designer

For instance, I love the ocean. I love the beach. So it's easy for me to pull that into almost any room because it will make me smile. It will feel refreshing. It will add a personal touch to any room. But that's me. Sometimes, people have things they collect, magazines they like, sports teams they follow, or charities they volunteer with and support. Think about your personal interests and about how to work those into your decor.

LET'S GET STARTED ON DESIGN POSSIBILITIES

Suggestion: First, read through this chapter completely, and then go back to work on and complete the worksheets.

Our strategy is to put together *three plans* of different options to achieve the result you want. Refer to your "Focus" worksheet #1 from chapter 1.

Create one option that is outrageous or out of the box, something that you really wouldn't normally consider. Stretch your thinking.

QUICK REVIEW

At the center of the Styleprint Design System is your wow room.

- It looks great!

- It feels fabulous!

- It functions as you wish.

There are four design areas involved in achieving the wow look:

1. light

2. color

3. arrangement/furnishings

4. details

DESIGN AREA #1: LIGHT

We begin with light because it affects everything. If there is no light, we can't see or do anything. Light is the foundation of everything in the space.

When a client does not like a room, I like to stand in it with them and have them tell me what they don't like about it. Many of their concerns trace back to the lighting. I listen both for concerns that might have simple, easy solutions and for concerns that call for higher-impact, more complex recommendations. Examples would be anything from adding more lighting fixtures to adding a window or enlarging a sliding door to better see the trees in the backyard.

First, assess the natural light for daytime. Is it adequate? Do you need to control the natural light? For instance, there might be too much sun coming in a window near a TV, producing glare. Or the sun might be directly in your eyes when dining at particular times of the year.

Natural light makes a real difference in the effect it has on furnishings, materials, textiles, and other surfaces in the room. Sunlight makes us feel good. Our bodies need it. It affects a person's mood and disposition. A lack of it has been shown to cause depression.

Next, think about cloudy days, wintertime, when there is less daylight, and evening activities. There are three types of artificial light for a room:

1. General: General lighting refers to the overall light in the room. Ceiling fixtures provide this.

2. Task: Task lighting refers to light for functions, such as cooking in the kitchen, reading a book, doing homework, sewing, applying makeup, shaving, and so on. Table, desk, and floor lamps are common sources of task lighting, as are pendant fixtures over an island or sink in the kitchen and light bars over a mirror in the bathroom.

3. Accent or mood: Accent lighting is used to highlight a particular area. Examples include lights over artwork on the wall, wall sconces, eyeball or recessed lights, and uplights behind plants and sculptures.

Lamp placement in a room will be tied to purpose. Scale the size of the lamp to the room and for the task. If you often perform a task in the room, such as knitting, sewing, or reading, you might consider adding a lamp on a side table at shoulder height. Often a light bar or track with halogen bulbs is used. This allows for flexibility, both through changing the direction of the bulbs and through dimmers. Dimmers give you more options so that you don't always have to light up the whole room.

It's a priority to have your home well lit. When you're selling a home, the real estate agent will go through the house and put on every light imaginable before prospective buyers arrive. That's done for a reason. Psychologically, it makes the house feel bigger and more inviting, and it highlights the space.

Trends in lighting change. When you assess a space to update it, changing the lighting fixtures can have a huge impact but is often overlooked. In today's kitchens we've gotten away from the old fluorescent rectangles and are trending toward pendants that hang down over an island or work area. Under-the-counter lighting is another option.

Photo courtesy of Therese Bush-Hilgar, Styleprint Designer

Another lighting trend is to put a chandelier in a bathroom, particularly in a master bath. This adds a touch of elegance and whimsy and makes the bathroom a little more intriguing. Occasionally use colored lighting but mainly for ambience. Use an uplight behind a plant, change the color according to the seasons, or bring attention to a particular color. You can also add room color with candles.

The type of bulbs you use also has impact. The trend is toward bulbs that have longer life and also provide a truer, whiter light. Even in fluorescents, there are bulbs that replicate daylight. They are a little more expensive, but use them wherever possible because they give a more natural light, which is more invigorating, causes less stress on the eyes, and makes people look better.

Photo courtesy of Karen Powell, Styleprint Creator and Designer

The wave of the future is programmable lighting. This can be as simple as cycling lights on and off using a timer that plugs into the wall or as advanced as a complete system that works through your smartphone. Programmable lighting allows you to save energy by turning things on and off remotely and also provides a safety function for your home.

Most rooms will have a combination of two or three types of lighting. This creates the most flexibility for the use of the space, and dimmer switches allow the level of light to be easily adjusted.

DESIGN AREA #2: COLOR

There are several ways to approach color in decorating. In the Styleprint Design System, we decorate first for use or function and then bring in look and feel.

Specify your color theme, its placement, and the medium used for the color application. These will be derived from how you want your room to feel. Identify three words to describe how you want the room to feel.

1.

2.

3.

If you want the room to feel larger, light, and airy, you will select lighter colors, as light colors recede and give the feeling of expanding space. If you want to make the room feel warm and cozy, less large, you will select deeper shades of color. For the warm feel, you will gravitate toward the warm tones of reds and yellows.

Are you looking for something that is relaxing? Blues and neutral tones will be your direction.

Do you want stimulation and contrast? That calls for a black-and-white combo: deeper shades of one color mixed with neutrals or lighter tints of the same color for a monochromatic effect. The chart on page

124 gives color selection tips and a brief look at the psychology of colors.

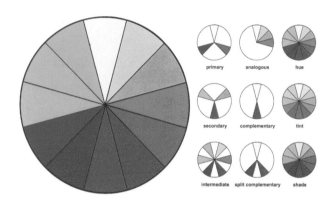

These color charts show the spectrum of colors, with intermediate shades between. Often, you see these presented in the color wheel format, illustrating how other colors are derived. For example, green is a combination of blue and yellow. A yellow green has more yellow than blue, and a blue green has more blue than yellow.

Photo courtesy of Amy Boesen, Styleprint Designer

When considering color in your decor, consider colors that you tend to favor. A great place to get a visual sense of this is your clothes closet. What colors are in there? Think back about color choices you have made in the past, and write them down. Do you see a pattern? Are there colors that represent the locations you've traveled to that make you smile? An alternative approach to selecting colors is to pick out a piece of art that you love and might want to see in the room. It could be a brand-new piece or something you already have. If you need something new for the room, go through an art catalog or look online to find something you love. You can build out the room from this.

Some online art sources are:

> www.surya.com: click on the wall decor tab.

> www.iconicpineapple.com: scroll down to shop by brands or categories.

> www.bentleyglobalarts.com: shop using the tabs at the top.

Placement of color is as important as selecting the actual colors. The following are guidelines. There are many situations in which you will break the rules, but you must first become an expert in using the rules.

Walls are the largest visual area in a room. Flooring is second. Furnishings are third. Good design dictates that you would not have one color for the walls, another color for the floors, and another color for the furnishings.

As a rule of thumb, the biggest area will have the least intense color and use the most intense color only as an accent.

Usually, a color does not appear in just one place. The exception would be to use a unique color to call attention to a particular area or piece to make it "pop," visually. It could be a vase on a table or a floral arrangement. It could be a piece of sculpture or something very dramatic that you want to be the focal point of the room.

As a rule of thumb, the biggest area will have the least intense color and use the most intense color only as an accent.

As an example of effective color placement, duplicate the wall color in the pillows on the sofa and in an accent piece on the table. Your eye would then travel from the wall to the pillows to the accent piece and around. It's pleasing to the eyes and is yet another piece of the puzzle in creating a wow room.

HOT AND COLD ON COLOR

Another color consideration is the use of "warm" tones versus "cool" tones. Cool colors have blue undertones whereas warm colors have yellow undertones. These are psychological temperatures. Cool colors include blue and cool whites. Colors with a red tinge, including yellows, are warm. Warm colors "advance"—they appear to come forward, have more prominence—while cool colors recede. If you have a small room and want it to look bigger, use cool colors instead of warm colors and lighter colors instead of intense colors.

On the other hand, the main challenge in decorating "great rooms"—those rooms that are large (20 feet by 25 feet and larger) with high ceilings, vaulted ceilings, or cathedral ceilings—is making them feel cozy. To make a great room seem cozy, we have to pull the room in through furniture placement, colors, and textures. Furniture groupings will pull conversation areas together, and textiles and textures with darker, deeper, richer colors will help cozy up this kind of space.

A PRIMER ON THE PSYCHOLOGY OF COLOR

The psychology of color is important, and entire books have been written and dedicated to just this subject. As a quick overview, let's look at the three primary colors: blue, red, and yellow.

Red embodies vitality, courage, and self-confidence. It signals us to pay attention. Of all the colors, red causes the most reaction. It's exciting. It causes our sense of smell to improve and increases our appetite. Usually, interiors done in red are dramatic and provocative.

Consider shades (the darker version of the hue) and tints (the lighter version of the hue) of red: bright red is the most energizing, dynamic, stimulating, aggressive color. Bright pink is happy, youthful, fun, and trendy. Light pink is romantic, soft, cute, and delicate. Dusty pink is cozy, subtle, and soft.

Yellow is thought of as joyful, outgoing, and friendly. It's bright, easily gets attention, and symbolizes energy and sunlight. It's associated with springtime, cheerfulness, and optimism. It's also cautious—as in yellow traffic lights—telling us to be careful, and it symbolizes safety because it's easy to see. It's also the color of ideas and dreams, and it stimulates creativity and confidence. It's an animating color for life, suggesting merriment and the psychological color of day. It's the most reflective of all the colors. It also stimulates the left side of the brain, so it promotes logical thinking and is a great color for home libraries and offices because of that. It helps you to absorb more information and stimulates the short-term memory. It's a great color for a room that lacks natural light.

In contrast to yellow, when bright yellow is used over large areas, it can make someone feel more anxious and can increase blood pressure. This refers to intensity, or saturation, which is the brightness or dullness of a color. Light yellow is cheerful, happy, sunny, warm, and sweet.

The third primary color is blue, which symbolizes knowledge, health, and truth. It's a color of constancy. It slows down the perception of time, creates a calming effect, and cools the body temperature. Blue is a distant and receding color. Interiors done in light blue will be pleasing and tranquil. Navy is a great color to use in business because it stands for truth, honesty, loyalty, and integrity. It can also be associated with formality. Blue is great for bedrooms because it helps you to feel cared for, and it eases loneliness. Splashes of deep blue engender meditation and make a room more spiritual. However, too much blue can be depressing, so you have to balance it.

Light blue is calm, quiet, peaceful, and cool. Sky blue is heavenly, happy, restful, and tranquil. Bright blue is electric, energetic, vibrant, happy, and dramatic.

When we combine two primary colors, we get secondary colors. The resulting hue will depend on the percentage of the colors being mixed and whether they are shades or tints of those colors. Mauve is a secondary color with more red than blue. It's soft and subdued, quiet, and sentimental. Burgundy is rich, elegant, expensive, and mature. Fuchsia is bright, hot, high-energy, and sensual. Brick red is earthy, strong, and warm and has a country note to it. Terra cotta is earthy, warm, wholesome, and welcoming.

Among secondary colors, orange represents happiness, confidence, and resourcefulness. Peach, which is a tint of orange, made of equal parts of red and yellow, harmonizes with almost anything. It's a great color to pull into a variety of situations. In comparison to apricot, peach will tend to have more red, and apricot more yellow.

Orange is a color for those who desire vitality and a sense of well-being. Orange helps to balance emotions and increase self-confidence and positive thinking. Adding orange or red to a yellow color scheme strengthens its impact.

Another secondary color, green, is a combination of blue and yellow and represents balance, self-control, and harmony. It's life, nature, calmness, and freshness. It's sensuous and alive, dependable, and steady. Green represents newness and regeneration; it's a healer. It's the most common color found in nature and has come to symbolize Mother Nature. The green movement is symbolic of ecology.

Green is a good color to decorate rooms for relaxation because it provides the space and time to rebalance. It's versatile and has limitless variations, depending on the colors it's mixed with. A greenish-yellow is lemony, tart, and fruity. Gold is warm, opulent, expensive, and prestigious. A teal blue is pleasing, rich, classy, and unique.

Turquoise is tropical and reminiscent of the ocean and jewelry. Aqua is cool, fresh, liquid, and healing.

Purple, also a secondary color, is a mix of red and blue. Purple symbolizes beauty, creativity, and spiritualism. It combines excitement and passion. It's also symbolic of leadership, respect, and wealth. It can reflect emotions from contemplative to regal and majestic. Historically, purple was the most expensive dye to make, so only the wealthy could afford it. It was the color of royalty and emperors since well before the Roman Empire. It's a sensual, spiritual, elegant, and mysterious color. It can be used in rooms for deep relaxation and meditation, as can green, or it can be used in any environment for an out-of-this-world feeling.

Splashes of purple in any social room will promote detachment and spiritual connection. It demands special attention. It's mystical and magical.

Everything from red-purple to deep plum, lavender, grape, and orchid are all in this family.

Black is an "uncolor," which means it's neutral. Black is characterized by what it's not; it lacks brightness, and it absorbs all light. It represents death and is the color of gloom. However, black is also strong, classic, and elegant and can be associated with sophistication and strength, mystery, and darkness. It can mean top of the line, or it can be the color of mourning. It symbolizes prudence and purity. Grey is the neutral zone between black and white.

White is another neutral, representing purity, cleanliness, and heavenliness. It makes a good background but isn't very interesting or particularly inviting. An all-white environment can cause glare and headaches if it's not broken up by other colors. Bright white is not recommended for floors or walls, but off-white is okay. White surfaces are recommended for ceilings to reflect maximum light and are essential with indirect lighting systems.

White is also a chameleon. It changes with each texture. The white of fur is not the same as the white of marble. Most whites that you see in decorating are not pure white. They have an undertone, whether it's blue for coolness or yellow for warmth. White will open up a space and can be used with every other color. It has many positives. It indicates delicacy, refinement, and sophistication; encourages precision; and reflects light. Interiors with a lot of white will be airy and bright. Pure white is associated with cleanliness and sterility. Innocent, silent, lightweight, and glistening are some of the adjectives that go along with it.

People's color preferences have a lot to do with their own personality and lifestyle.

People have preferences for color. Some people like blue; others don't. Rarely will someone not like any of the hues of a particular color. For example, there will be shades or tints of blue that people prefer or dislike.

People's color preferences have a lot to do with their own personality and lifestyle.

If you think of people who are very high energy, always on the go, with a lot of enthusiasm about life, you might expect their home to be filled with bright, vivid colors. And yet, when you see their house, it might lean toward calm, neutral, and serene colors. This could simply be because they have a high-energy job, and when they go home, their focus is on relaxation and rejuvenation. The colors must support that.

In creating your wow decor, pull all these ingredients together. Create a color palette uniquely for you, for a room, and for your home. For instance, the flooring in your home, no matter what material it is (be it carpet, hardwood, or tile), is of a particular color. That color becomes a thread that will be pulled into all of the other color themes within your home.

The color theme will be dispersed throughout the room. Everything has color: paint, wall coverings, textiles, floor finishes, cabinetry, countertops, and light fixtures. All of these items and their colors need to be pulled together so that they create continuity within all of the pieces of decor that make up the room. It's like pulling together an orchestra of many different instruments. We don't want one section of jazz and another of rock and roll, because, together, they will only sound like noise. The same can happen with colors. They can all look very disjointed and dysfunctional if they don't flow.

THE STYLEPRINT® DESIGN SYSTEM
TECHNICAL DÉCOR INFO: TIPS ABOUT
COLOR SELECTION

Terms:

Hue: color

Saturation: purity of a hue; most intense = saturated; muted = black, gray, or complimentary color added

Value: lightness or darkness of a color

Intensity: how dark or light the color is

Primary colors: red, blue, yellow

Secondary colors: Green, orange, violet

Color Psychology:

Blue: Calmness/serenity; Curbs appetite; Associated with water and peace; People are more productive in blue rooms (most used color for offices); Color most preferred by men

Yellow: Cheerful/warm/bright; Increases metabolism; Energy; Makes babies cry; May cause eye strain; Caution

Red: Evokes strong emotions; Encourages appetite; Passion/intensity; Red roses symbolize love

Green: Tranquility and health; Money; Nature

Orange: Excitement/enthusiasm; Warmth; Used to draw attention

Lavender: Calms the nerves/allows relaxation; Royalty/wealth; Success; Wisdom

Color Schemes:
Monochromatic: shades and tints of one color plus neutrals. **Complimentary**: colors that are opposite on the color wheel. **Triad**: three colors equally spaced on the color wheel. **Analogous**: three or more colors side-by-side on the color wheel.

Color Mix:
Dominant: 60%; walls, flooring, or fabric backgrounds
Secondary: 30% found throughout the room in fabrics, art, and accessories
Accent: 10% used minimally to provide the "pop" in the room

*Colors are to be used in at least 3 places and on two levels; Levels of the room: floor level, eye level, and mid level.

Basic Tips:
People are drawn to intensities
Color fan decks are usually arranged from left to right with saturation
Paint colors: Are best selected at noon to get the truest color representation—it will vary throughout the day; Colors will look different on every wall; Will look darker on the wall than on the paint fan swatch: Will dry darker than it goes on—Reds take three days to cure for true color.
Ceilings do not have to be white
Accent colors draw attention to architectural features

Color in and of itself is free when you purchase something; the item happens to come in a color. When you buy a gallon of paint, you're getting a gallon of paint regardless of its color. Take advantage of it.

WHEN NEUTRAL IS A NO-NO

Sometimes, people go overboard on neutrals because they're afraid of color. "Color phobia" is the number-one fear in decorating. Selecting all neutrals doesn't mean that you're doing a great job decorating. You must use neutrals in the proper proportions and add color where you need it. Otherwise, you will end up with a blah room. You will walk into it and say, "There's nothing special to this room."

If you think you're saving yourself from making a color mistake by going all-neutral, think again. An all-neutral color scheme is just as intricate to pull off as is any other color scheme. Placement and proportions delineate how the neutral colors are carried into the room and where.

If you are thinking of preparing your home to sell, do not be afraid to use color. If you use it well, it can help sell the home. Your home will be more attractive. We find that a home sells closer to the asking price and sells more quickly when it's well decorated—and that includes great use of color. A home decorated according to the principles and elements of good design is much more attractive than a home that is devoid of color, that has no personality. Good design, even if it's not your own personal style, trumps the absence of color.

A color theme usually consists of one, two, or three colors with varying degrees of intensity (shades and tints). As a general guideline, the lower-intensity color should cover more space, and the bolder color should be the accent, occupying the smallest amount of space.

Use of one color is a monochromatic theme, utilizing shades and tints of the one color: from light to medium to dark. A two-color theme will consist of one as the dominant color and the other as the secondary and accent sprinkled around the room. The accent would be the deeper tint of the color. An example would be a complementary color scheme where the two colors are opposite each other on the color wheel: blue with orange or orange with blue; red with green or pink with aqua; yellow with purple or purple with gold.

One version of three colors is known as an analogous color scheme comprised of three colors next to each other on the color wheel. An example of this: blues, greens, and yellows in varying degrees of mixing and shades and tints of each color. This scheme can be a lot of fun to work with, as there are almost limitless possibilities.

Placement of color is a critical part of getting things right with decorating. When you size up a room, there are three levels: eye level, floor level, and midlevel. The eye level has to do with the walls: the color of the walls, window treatments, artwork, and fixtures. The floor level is everything that you walk on. The midlevel is what is in the middle of the room: the furnishings and the accents, such as pillows, throws, accessories, florals, and greenery. When placing color in a room, be sure to have the color flow in a curved fashion. To do that, you will, typically, include a color on two levels in at least three places. That way your eye moves easily among the objects in the room. It's a pleasant, restful experience for your eyes.

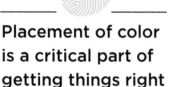

Placement of color is a critical part of getting things right with decorating.

Next, from your color theme, determine which colors will fulfill the roles of

- dominant (60 percent of the room)

- secondary (30 percent of the room)

- accent (10 percent of the room)

The dominant role will be for the main color, which will cover more of the space proportionately. It will encompass the walls and possibly the floor and may be included in some of the furnishings. The secondary color may cover the flooring or be part of it and may be part of the furnishings and window treatments. The accent color will appear as highlights in appropriate places, such as one of the colors in the floral arrangement, in the upholstery pattern, in the pillows, or in the trim on any of the textiles in the room.

To keep this simple: If you elect to use three colors, one color will, typically, be on the walls and floors, another color will be on the furnishings, and another color will be an accent, possibly in the art, the textiles, the pattern on the sofa, the accessories, and/or the flooring (such as a small part of a pattern in an area rug). Intermingled will be neutral colors (beiges, whites, blacks, and grays). You should also scatter the colors around the room.

As you translate the color palette into the room, you may use a patterned textile or wall covering that will carry more than one color. Using patterns in a room allows you to create interest and to intermingle the colors of your theme. Patterns come in three sizes, and there are rules about mixing them. The three sizes are referred to as random, regulated, and miniprints. Random patterns are usually large-scale with a repeat of over 20 inches. Regulated patterns are those that repeat in a regimented way. Examples are stripes and diamond or harlequin patterns. These will, typically, have a repeat of somewhere between 7 and 20 inches. Miniprints are those with a repeat of less than 7 inches. Note that, sometimes, the repeat is so small it can look like a solid color when viewed from a distance.

All three categories of patterns may be used together in a room with the following criteria:

1. The color theme is consistent. This means that the colors are mixed among the patterns.

2. Neutrals and solid colors are used as transition between the patterns.

3. As a general guideline, the random pattern (largest scale of pattern) is used on the largest area such as the walls or the sofa. This is not always the case; however, it is a good place to begin.

   One example: the wall covering or sofa would be a large-scale pattern; the medium-size pattern (regulated)—possibly a stripe— would be placed in the window treatment, pillows, or a side chair; and the smallest pattern (miniprint) as part of the top treatment, pillows, or area rug.

4. Patterns are best spread throughout the room on the different levels (eye, mid, and floor) for balance and visual appeal.

Photo courtesy of Therese Bush-Hilgar, Styleprint Designer

Wall coverings are an underused method of incorporating color in a room.

One of the biggest myths in decorating is that if you use wallpaper, you are stuck with it. "Stuck" is a relative term. Selecting a wall covering doesn't mean you're forever stuck with the way the room looks. You can alter the look by changing out some of the specific things in the room.

Photo courtesy of Bonnie Peet, Styleprint Designer, Hambley Team

A benefit of a wall covering is that it lasts longer than paint, so when you look at the dollar investment, it's very cost effective. If the wall covering is put up properly and professionally, you're not going to need to redo it as frequently as you would paint. If you think you might get tired of something, you might not be making the right choice to begin with. In terms of your decorating dollars, a wall covering will give you far more ambience and style than anything else you can put in the room. It will last three to four times as long as paint. The

Wall coverings are an underused method of incorporating color in a room.

initial outlay may be slightly more for the wall covering and installation. However, the difference in the cost of paint versus wall covering is not drastic, considering the longevity of a wall covering; it pays for itself over time.

Wall covering has come a long way. I think of it as a hidden treasure.

And it's easy to change the look of a room by changing out the window treatments, the area rug, the table linens, or pillows. In a dining room, the fabric of the chair seats

Wall covering has come a long way. I think of it as a hidden treasure.

and other upholstered pieces can easily be modified. In this way you can retain the wall covering, yet still create a new look and feel.

LIVENING UP A ROOM WITH WALL COVERINGS

Using a wall covering doesn't mean you have to cover all four walls. In a bedroom it could just be on the wall behind the bed. A nice headboard can extend that look and make the entire wall a focal point, heightening the appeal. Or the covering could be on all four walls and the ceiling as well. (A great place to do that is in a powder room.) This adds a nice touch to the look and feel of a room. If you have a room with a vaulted or cathedral ceiling, having a wall covering going up the ceiling adds to the visual impact of the room.

If a room has an architectural feature that you want to highlight, think about how wallpaper could complement it. Imagine pairing up a wall covering with lighting, such as a chandelier, in a master bath or powder room. This is the epitome of small indulgences.

SETTING THE TONE

Wall covering can also provide the inspiration for a room's decor. In my dining room the wallpaper was the inspiration for the rest of the room. In other scenarios the inspiration can be a fabric that becomes part of the furniture, pillows, or window treatments.

You need to do this with care to make sure that everything blends and doesn't fight. The basis for this analysis will be your color plan: the distribution of that color and the pattern mix. You'll want to have samples or pictures of all the elements you select for your plan in each option. Lay them out to look at them together. There is even computer software today that shows your samples in a room so that you can get a better idea of how they will actually look.

To recap: when applying your color theme to the room, you must consider:

- where it will be placed;

- what its material is and how it's used (is it a textile pattern, wall covering, rug, window treatment?);

- the percentage of use;

- the color intensity in relation to other colors; and

- intermixing neutral tones to assist with transition and color enhancement.

DESIGN AREA #3: ARRANGEMENT/ FURNISHINGS

Placement of your furnishings is a top priority. The furniture must be placed so that you can easily move about the room, have conversations, watch TV, or otherwise function as you desire. A quick tip to assist in getting the room arrangement right is to divide the room into quadrants (see diagram). Analyze each quadrant for visual weight:

- architectural features
- furnishings

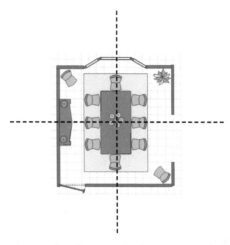

The visual weight for good design is balanced and equal. All four quadrants must have equal weight of features and furnishings combined (see illustration).

The following are key space allowances to consider when planning the furnishings in a room:

- A conversation area is approximately eight feet, measuring from the front of the sofa to the front of a chair. Less than this and you will feel cramped; more will have you feeling you need to shout to converse.

- Leave 18 inches between the coffee table and the sofa.

- Viewing distance for a TV will depend on its size. The instructions for most large-screen TVs specify an appropriate distance for maximum viewing pleasure. Be sure to measure this out so that the TV will work optimally in your space.

For a dining room or kitchen table, you need three feet beyond the table to allow someone sitting in the chair to slide out from the table and get out of the chair.

MIXING TEXTURES

You can also mix textures in a room. A silk fabric has a different texture from that of cotton or linen or wool. Flat, shiny fabrics are more formal than those that have more texture. Are you looking for a casual feel or something more formal? This may be determined by the function of the room and personal preferences. Remember this is all about people having a room that they love, that speaks to them and invites them in.

FABRIC-COVERED FURNISHINGS

Textiles have come a long way. Many of them today are very durable and forgiving. They are treated for stain resistance so if something spills, it's easily cleaned up. Have extra fabric protection put on the material before it's delivered. It's an extra layer of insurance and comes with an 800 number to call if you're not sure how to get a stain out.

This is important because the rooms in your home are rooms to be lived in. They need to feel good and look good, but they can't just look good for the first week. They have to look good for many years. That's good design. Consider who will be using the room. If the room users are aging, seat height and the firmness of the seat cushions are primary considerations.

It's difficult for older people to sit down in and stand up from really low seating. Down-filled cushions are cushy and comfy, but it's harder to get up from them. Older people need something firmer. Seating also has to be the proper height so that it hits the back of the knees easily. And make sure there is a nice arm on the sofa to help sitters stand up.

MULTITASK ACTIVITY ROOMS

Some really big family rooms must be decorated in sections. There may be a seating area in front of the TV and fireplace, a game table with chairs in another part of the room, and a desk or armoire in another section. Someone could be doing homework on a computer at the desk while others play cards or do a puzzle at the game table.

Similarly, when decorating bedrooms, all activities need to be considered. In their bedrooms, children might need a desk in addition to their bed. If they are doing homework at the desk, be sure the lighting is conducive for that. Certainly, you want a desk light as well as general lighting. If the kids listen to music in their room, where will you put the equipment? Years ago that meant a big stereo system, but now people keep their music on an iPod or smartphone. They just need space for a docking station and speakers and sufficient outlets.

TODAY'S MASTER BEDROOMS ARE MULTIPURPOSE ROOMS

Master bedrooms today can be quite large, with exercise areas, a desk, and maybe a seating area where the adults can just sit, talk, or read. They might have a TV near the bed or mounted on a wall or a ceiling.

Working electronics into a room setting—TV, audio, and all the other devices we can't seem to live without today—is another reality for us to design into a room. What are the pieces that need to be included, and how many? Where do they need to be? And how will we get power to them? Sometimes clients decide they want a room that is electronics-free or prefer to use iPads or other portable devices that can be used anywhere in the house with a wireless connection. They will still require a place for recharging. Know this and build out from there.

THE STYLEPRINT® DESIGN SYSTEM
TECHNICAL DÉCOR INFO: THINGS TO THINK
ABOUT AND PLAN FOR

As you prepare to arrange your room for function, it is time to think beyond the activities of the room and consider what else is needed to support you and your lifestyle.

Will you be wanting to charge any of your devices?

Mobile phone

iPad, tablet, or laptop

Headset

Fitbit

Other

If so, you will need outlets or a wifi charging device, and a space to place them on, as well as a place to store cords.

What else is needed in the room?

Storage or display for a collection?

Reading material—magazines/catalogs or books?

Desk accessories—pad/pen/pencil/letter opener/scissors

Jewelry/watch tray

Place for keys

Mail—incoming and outgoing

Packages/packets/backpacks/briefcases for delivery (dry cleaners, etc) or daily event

Pet bed/toys/leashes

Other—fill in your personal items

DESIGN AREA #4: DETAILS

After the major pieces are specified and placed, consider the finishing details. Art, area rugs, window treatments, accessories, greenery, and florals all add to the personalization of the room and make the room come to life.

Of these, art can have the most impact simply because its selection is totally a matter of personal taste and style. In addition, wall accessories have a dramatic impact on a room's balance. Without something on the walls, the furniture in a room looks unfinished. Procurement and installation of wall art will even enhance the room before the major furnishing pieces have been purchased, delivered, and set up.

The subject of the art you select will elicit certain feelings when you enter the room, and you want to be sure to align the piece with the feelings you want your room to create. Do you want your room to be restful or exciting, stimulating or peaceful? Go back to the words you used at the beginning of this chapter to describe how you want to feel in this room.

List three feelings for your room:

1.

2.

3.

Review these words. Are they still valid? Or are you changing direction? It happens. Better to have it happen now while you are planning. It will save you money, time, and disappointment.

For example, some people love a particular scene, possibly from a place they have traveled to, while others derive enjoyment from a floral painting, and still others are drawn to an abstract painting of color, texture, and geometric shapes. Look at many, and choose a few that you like. Ultimately, the colors, size, matting, and framing of the art will coordinate with your space and the textiles and patterns that you have chosen. When all that is taken into account, one of your selections may fit better than the others for this room plan. Also, consider placement of the art within the room:

- Start with the largest wall. The art on this wall will draw your eye to the wall and help to fill up the space—and also help to balance the visual weight of the room.

- Hang artwork with the center of the picture at eye level.

- Use mirrors to reflect and expand space; always be conscious of what a mirror reflects, and be sure it's pleasing.

- Some walls may be prime space for a grouping of two or more pieces. They can be equal in size or they can vary, for interest. Additionally, the matting and framing are not required to be alike. Something must be similar across the group (for example, the color or the theme of the art), but it can be whimsical to vary the selection and the grouping.

- As a guideline, use ratios of 2:3 or 3:5 in determining the amount of wall space to cover with art. A five-foot sofa would suggest that three feet of the wall behind the sofa be covered with artworks placed 4 to 12 inches above the back of the sofa.

- When hanging art in a grouping or in pairs, center the pieces on an imaginary vertical or horizontal line—not a diagonal. A diagonal is appropriate when you are drawing the eye to a higher place, such as the top of a stairway.

- In groupings, balance the color of the art—light and dark—so that it's interspersed throughout the grouping and not all light or dark on one side. This goes back to the visual weight, with dark being perceived as heavier.

- Space between individual pieces of wall decor should be similar, with a minimum of one to three inches.

After art, we consider the next finishing detail, area rugs, which serve several purposes:

- functioning as art for the floor (this is particularly beneficial when you do not have much wall space for art or you have a large room and you want to bring in some interest)

- defining a conversation area in a large room

- covering up a floor that is in poor condition

- warming up flooring that has a cold look and feel

- absorbing noise

There are a multitude of area rug constructions, patterns, styles, and durability levels to choose from. Some come in standard sizes, and others can be customized. The following factors will contribute to the investment level and longevity of the rug. Consider them when determining your criteria.

- Does it need to be durable?

- Is it a room that gets a lot of use?

- Is there direct sunlight?

- Are there kids?

- Are there pets?

- Other considerations?

Universal design—the principles of designing environments accessible to all people—would suggest *not* using area rugs as the inhabitants age, because people may trip over them, and they also act as deterrents to using a wheelchair or walker.

The next finishing detail, window treatments and coverings, can do much to enhance your room's personality.

Window coverings (shades, blinds, and shutters) are practical for privacy, for energy conservation, or for light control. In some instances, you may not need a covering for privacy, because you live in an area where neighbors are not close, but the "blackness" of the window at night may not be to your liking. Window treatments, on the other hand, draw attention to the window, soften the look of the room, and can add a level of panache. They can be simple or multilayered.

The trend today is away from the complex and toward the simple. The most requested treatments are a simple decorative top over a shade or blind or drapery panels on a decorative rod. This does not mean that one size or one look fits all. On the contrary, size does matter, and there is no such thing as a standard look. With millions of textiles, colors, and patterns available, there is never a need to have any one window treatment duplicated anywhere else on the planet. This is truly an area on which to put your personal touch—your Styleprint.

Among the finishing details, greenery and florals are pieces that literally bring life into a room. If you are looking for easy care and maintenance, go faux. The creation of faux greenery and florals has come a long way from the plastic flowers of our heritage, or if you have a green thumb and the time to care for your inside garden, using live plants is always a good choice. There is really no excuse not to include greenery and florals in some form … and their presence speaks volumes. You will want a minimum of three in a room.

The last of the finishing touches, the accessories— the personal photos, candles, artifacts, collections, vases, figurines, and various other display items—are the jewels of your decor and the ultimate in personal-izing your space. As with all things in decor, there is an art and a science to these finishing touches. And there is a fine line between tasteful and cluttered.

First, here is what not to do. Do not overwhelm the room with personal photos and mementos. Select the highlights, and strategically place them in areas of prominence as background or intermingled with other items. Often a gallery wall of a collection of photos or an arrangement of photos on a table will do nicely. Do not overdo. Highlight that which is most important. This is truly an "editing" function. Decide on the ones that are most important, and put the others elsewhere. One of the things I like to do is to make an annual family photo book using Shutterfly online (www. shutterfly.com). This way, I recap the year with the best photos and, together, those become a coffee table book. From that collection, I periodically select a few photos to change out other photos around the house.

Another tip for accessories is to create a treasure box or treasure trunk with a few things from the year. Edit these down so that you are not overwhelmed. After all, what will you really do with everything you keep? No one else will be as enamored with your stuff as you are, and is it so valuable that you want to pay to store it? Edit, edit, edit …

Also, identify a theme for your accessories, and determine whether there is some seasonality to them. Do you like to change out your decor for holidays? And don't forget to include potpourri or a variety of scented candles in your decor. Involving all of the senses is an important step and one that is often overlooked in decorating. For your sense of taste, you might have a dish of mints or chocolates prominently displayed. One word of caution: consider pets and small children and be mindful of who has easy access.

When placing accessories, odd numbers fair better visually than even numbers. So use three candles or a grouping of three, five, or seven items on the mantel instead of two or four.

Worksheet #3 ("Your Styleprint Specifics")—one for each of three options—is your summary of this chapter and where you apply what you have learned. With each worksheet, include samples or photos of your selections so that you can lay them all out together and review.

- How do they look?

- How do they feel?

- Do they function?

Present them to others. What questions do they have? Can you visualize the room? What questions do you have?

Which option do you like best? If others are involved in the decorating design of the room, have them weigh in. You may even find you like a hybrid of the plans, a combination of items from two or three of the plans. Make a selection ... or not. If it's not working for you, go back to your "Focus" and "Evaluation" worksheets. What did you miss or skip over? Tweak your plans. If there is one that makes you smile, congratulations! You have created your Styleprint design!

CHAPTER FOUR

STEP 4: A MANAGED MAKEOVER

You have identified your decor goals.

You have evaluated your space.

You have determined the resources for this project.

You have created plans and selected one.

The managed makeover is next.

Now is the time to make it happen, the time to wave our magic wand and say, "Abracadabra! Transform this room into the finished result!"

And that's what it will be like...almost. Worksheet #4 ("Your Action Plan", found in the Appendix) for the managed makeover will be your guide throughout this chapter. In this worksheet, you will list all of the actions to be taken and items to be purchased, removed, or donated.

There is a sequencing of events that has to happen with the makeover to make this easy. If not followed, it becomes difficult. If you are changing the carpeting, for example, you will first need to remove the furniture and install the new carpet. Painting is done before new flooring is installed. Your decor makeover is orchestrated and choreographed so that it flows and makes sense. Allow ample time to coordinate these varying miniprojects in your plan. Use the worksheet to prioritize projects and record target dates for completion.

There may be items to donate. You might be replacing a piece of furniture that is still in decent condition so that someone else can benefit from it. There are many local organizations for this. A few sources are:

- Satruck.org: The Salvation Army Family Stores will pick up furniture.

- Goodwill.org: drop off or some locations will pick up; call local Goodwill for details.

- Pickupplease.org will pick up furniture; benefits a veterans organization.

- Check out local thrift shops.

As an alternative to donating items, you could consider selling your furnishings. You could do this through (to offer a few suggestions—there are many more):

- Ebay
- Craigslist

- Furniture.about.com
- Local consignment stores
- Community tag sales/flea markets

When you begin decorating or redecorating, you won't want to be without furniture for long. Do not remove the things you don't want to keep until "Your Action Plan" allows their convenient removal. That is a job in itself—choreographing *this* to make sure *that* happens and *then* the next, in the right order. Make sure that events flow nicely and without much lag time between and that someone does not drop the ball. That can be frustrating, as it may hold up progress on the entire project.

Sometimes, you will do things in stages because of budget, time frame, or availability of resources. Review your plans to ensure that you get the first things done first, and then fill in with other things.

DECORATING BY THE NUMBERS

Now you're ready to set up your room, adding the finishing touches. You are almost done, so don't stop now! These final enhancements can make the difference between the wow room you wanted in the beginning and "It's nice."

Remember to refer back to your "Action Plan," Worksheet #4. You thought all of this out. Now is the time to execute.

When grouping accessories in a room, such as on a table or mantel, odd numbers are the way to go. The same goes for pillows. Why odd numbers? It's a geometric thing, but the bottom line is that odd-number groupings always look better. That's why candles often come in sets of three. So when you're accessorizing, use one or three or five or seven items. When you want one of those items to be highlighted, put it more or less in the middle of the group (but actually a little *above* the middle).

Grouped accessories don't all have to be the same thing or the same color, but they do need to relate. Group them together so that they look as if they are a unit. You could put a candle, a vase, and a frame together as a grouping on a mantel.

Photo courtesy of Amy Boesen, Styleprint Designer

When it comes to furnishings and accessories, it's important to find a balance between functionality and space. Functionality is also a personal expression of what people do in the room and how they do it, whether it's formal, informal, or in between. This is where clients' preferences override all else, highlighting their unique personality.

When it comes to furnishings and accessories, the key consideration involves functionality versus space.

Now that all of the work is done, the setup is complete.

- How does it look?

- How does it feel?

- Does it have the functionality you were looking for?

Declare success when you feel yourself smile at the transformation in your space. Are you excited about it? Have you fallen in love with your home all over again? If yes, you have rediscovered its magic!

When it comes to furnishings and accessories, the key consideration involves functionality versus space.

Taking time to redo your decor revitalizes you, helping you feel better about something you were not feeling great about before.

CHAPTER FIVE

STEP 5: THE STYLEPRINT SHOWCASE

The fifth and final step is the Styleprint showcase. This is really the easy part. Everything has been done. The room is complete; it looks good, it feels good, and it functions. Now it's time to enjoy!

Three final things:

1. Worksheet #5 is "Your Decor Experience Review" (see Appendix). Rate your project on how well it accomplishes your original vision. A rating of one equals "not at all," and a rating of five equals "Wow! It exceeds my expectations."

2. Step back and look at the room with a critical design eye. Are there any last-minute changes? Do you need to move an accessory? Rearrange pillows? Do anything else that would enhance the look, feel, or function of the room?

3. Invite someone over to have a chat, and enjoy a glass of wine or iced tea in your new space, or just take your shoes off and admire.

When you walk into a room that is decorated well, even if it's not decorated in your personal style, it's going to give you a good feeling, and you will find it easy to appreciate. When you walk into a room that is decorated in your style but does not follow good design principles, it will be unsettling, and you won't be happy in it. You might enter the room, but you won't want to stay.

Now that you have experienced how to Styleprint a room, take a break and then plan to evaluate each room. Ask yourself which rooms you like to spend time in and which rooms you avoid. If you find yourself avoiding some rooms, maybe it's just that they aren't Styleprinted. That doesn't mean your home has to have a total redo, but perhaps there are a couple of things you can do to pull it together.

It pays to create spaces that are pleasing and inviting to those who live in the house.

The Styleprint Design System results in your unique combination of

- light,

- color,

- room arrangement/furnishings,

- patterns/solid/texture finishes and textiles,

- accessorizing,

- personal touches, and

- something for all the senses.

A Styleprinted room

- is visually pleasing;

- feels great … invites you in and begs you to stay;

- functions for what you need; and

- is all about you!

It's important to note that when you have taken the time to go through the exercises—to think, analyze, evaluate, prioritize, plan, and implement—you may not end up with perfection, a perfect ten. And that is okay! Decorating and keeping your space so that those who live in it love it, it supports your lives, and

It pays to create spaces that are pleasing and inviting to those who live in the house.

it feels like "you" is a fluid process. Some of it may change seasonally, some of it may change every year or two (like updating personal photos and accessories), and some of it may just wear out and need to be replaced. What is most important is that your space brings a smile to your face. We are looking to increase your satisfaction with your space to a much higher level: the level of delight.

This process has been a labor of love; it's your space, and it's important that it reflects you. With that being said, unless you want to do this professionally, it probably isn't something you want to continually have on your mind, with a never-ending stream of to-dos. So decide when you will focus on decorating, when you will do projects, and when to say, "Enough! Save it for the next project."

As you progress through life's stages and memorable events, so will your tastes in decor and your needs, because your space is an outward reflection of you. Embrace it—and enjoy it.

Love the space you are in!

 *FINAL THOUGHTS*

We would love to hear from you.

Do you have questions?

Have you Styleprinted a room? Please email photos and worksheets.

How did this book help you?

You can reach us at info@styleprintdesignsystem.com

 *A P P E N D I X*

WORKSHEET #1:
FOCUS STEP

Most decorating starts with something that is either "not right" or "missing."

This is all part of the preliminary conversation—to identify the level of interaction.

Take photos of room.

Identify the project:

Simple

↑

    Semi-Redo Room
    (1-3 items involved)

    Redo Entire Room

    Redo Entire Home

↓

Complex

WHAT do you want to accomplish?

WHY do you want to make this change?

Your VISION of the completed project. What does it look like?

Specifics:

1.

2.

3.

4.

5.

Options

Taking action will result in...

OR if you choose no action—what's the result?

WORKSHEET #2:
EVALUATE YOUR SPACE:
DECOR & YOU MASTER PLAN
INVESTMENT WORKSHEET

Category	What's Working	What Needs Replacing/ Missing	Investment Range
Overall Impression of Your Room			
Function			
Lighting			
Color Theme			
Floor Planning & Accessibility			
Walls			
Floors			
Ceiling			
Furniture			

Category	What's Working	What Needs Replacing/ Missing	Investment Range
Window Treatments			
Wall Art			
Accessories			
Storage			
Total Investment Range:			

WORKSHEET #3:

YOUR STYLEPRINT SPECIFICS

Prepare one sheet for each option, recommended three options.

Option _____   Room/Project:

Brief description of how you want the room to:

Look:

Feel:

Function:

Lighting:

As is:

Change/Add:

Color theme:

Dominant: Placement:

Secondary: Placement:

Accent: Placement:

Room Arrangement (include layouts):

As is:

Change/Add:

Walls:

As is:

Change/Add:

Floors:

As is:

Change/Add:

Ceiling:

As is:

Change/Add:

Furniture—upholstered:

As is:

Change/Add:

Furniture—case goods:

As is:

Change/Add:

Window treatments and coverings (soft and hard):

As is:

Change/Add:

Wall Art:

As is:

Change/Add:

Accessories:

As is:

Change/Add:

Storage:

As is:

Change/Add:

** Include samples/photos

Note colors/patterns (scale of pattern: mini, regulated, random) and texture use

INVESTMENT $

WORKSHEET #4:
ACTION PLAN

Create your action plan. Be sure to take photos at the beginning and end of each project.

Select Specific Items/ Actions	Order/ Schedule	Delivered/ Installed	Task Completed
1.			
2.			
3.			
4.			
5.			

WORKSHEET #5:

YOUR DECOR EXPERIENCE REVIEW

Rate your experience and results on a scale of 1-5.
1 = not at all   5 = WOW! Exceeds expectations

Does it meet your completed vision criteria?

1   2   3   4   5

Did it solve your decorating dilemma?

1   2   3   4   5

What's working?

What's not?

What could you have done differently to achieve a better outcome?

Is additional action required?

THE STYLEPRINT® DESIGN SYSTEM

www.ingramcontent.com/pod-product-compliance
Lightning Source LLC
Jackson TN
JSHW041549131224
75386JS00024B/490